Praise for *Forever Home*

Anh Lin has written a book that will have readers rejoicing in the powerful testimony of triumph over trauma and hurt. You will find yourself nodding along to biblical truths while being gently led to self-reflection.

Wendy Lau, interior stylist and digital creator @TheKWendyHome

The journey of healing isn't linear and is often extremely painful. It requires a breaking and a cleaning out of the heart to rebuild a story that leaves a legacy of hope and resilience. Anh Lin has crafted a book that can help you create a story you can be proud of. I challenge you to dig deep into this book and the painful parts of your story so you and God can rebuild something beautiful together. I assure you it will be worth it.

Toni Collier, speaker, podcast host, and
author of *Brave Enough to Be Broken*

Forever Home is a heartfelt book that takes readers on an honest and vulnerable journey of healing from trauma. Through personal and touching stories, including the reconstruction of her relationship with her mom, Anh Lin shares an empowering story of rebirth, renewal, and rediscovery of one's self-worth. With educational insights into psychology and therapy, along with practical journaling prompts, this book is a transformative guide to rebuilding oneself from within.

Aileen Xu, creator @lavendaire and the *Artist of Life* workbook

A beautifully written, inspiring debut book comes from Anh Lin, who personally invites you into her past traumas and onto her healing journey of rebuilding a safe haven, a forever home that is built on the strong foundation of Jesus' love. Her words are tender yet powerful. She speaks directly to healing your broken past and guides you with insightful spiritual and psychological tools to take tangible steps of ultimately finding your very own forever home.

Lena Kang, digital creator and influencer @Lenaxstyle

Forever Home is a powerful memoir that illuminates the path to healing from trauma and finding solace through God's love, mercy, and grace. Through her personal journey, Anh Lin reveals the profound truth that your trauma can serve as a catalyst for drawing closer to your forever home—a place of healing, peace, and divine love. This book offers a transformative message of hope, inspiring you to embrace your own journey of healing through insightful questions, scientific studies, and practical application.

Maya Lee, digital creator and influencer @mayaleex3

Anh Lin wants to help you renovate your heart. *Forever Home* will help you build a new foundation for your life.

Heather Thompson Day, author of *I'll See You Tomorrow*

Forever
Home

Forever Home

moving beyond brokenness to build a strong and beautiful life

Anh Lin

ZONDERVAN
BOOKS

ZONDERVAN BOOKS

Forever Home
Copyright © 2023 by Anh Lin

Requests for information should be addressed to:
Zondervan, *3900 Sparks Dr. SE, Grand Rapids, Michigan 49546*

Zondervan titles may be purchased in bulk for educational, business, fundraising, or sales promotional use. For information, please email SpecialMarkets@Zondervan.com.

ISBN 978-0-310-36638-6 (audio)

Library of Congress Cataloging-in-Publication Data

Names: Lin, Anh, 1992- author.
Title: Forever home : moving beyond brokenness to build a strong and beautiful life / Anh Lin.
Description: Grand Rapids : Zondervan, 2023.
Identifiers: LCCN 2023015016 (print) | LCCN 2023015017 (ebook) | ISBN 9780310366362 (hardcover) | ISBN 9780310366379 (ebook)
Subjects: LCSH: Lin, Anh, 1992- | Suffering—Religious aspects—Christianity. | Psychic trauma—Religious aspects—Christianity | BISAC: RELIGION / Christian Living / Personal Growth | RELIGION / Christian Living / Inspirational
Classification: LCC BV4909 .L55 2023 (print) | LCC BV4909 (ebook) | DDC 248.8/6—dc23 /eng/20230526
LC record available at https://lccn.loc.gov/2023015016
LC ebook record available at https://lccn.loc.gov/2023015017

Cover design: Curt Diepenhorst
Cover illustration: mariamsol_ms / Shutterstock
Interior photos: © Anh Lin
Interior design: Denise Froehlich

Printed in the United States of America

23 24 25 26 27 LBC 5 4 3 2 1

To my husband—
whose endless acts of service
speak louder than words ever could.
Thank you for loving me so well
despite my many shortcomings.
May God allow us to continue healing together
until the day of glorification.

Contents

Introduction

The Demolition

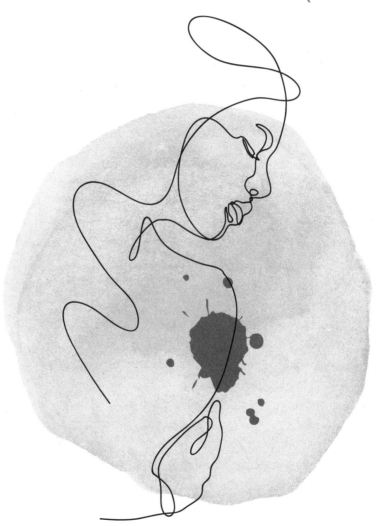

I took a deep inhale, swung the door open with one hand, and covered my mouth with the other. Our home looked like an apocalyptic scene—tiles were broken, walls were smashed in, and everything was covered in a revolting film of grime. Fractured pieces of concrete crunched beneath my feet as I made my way into what used to be our family room. Now it just looked like a dusty, decrepit building that had been abandoned in a natural disaster.

I was told by my contractors that the demolition phase would look severe, but to see it in person was overwhelming. The entire space seemed so beyond repair that I couldn't imagine how anyone would be able to clean it up, let alone live inside it. *How did I get here?* I thought to myself. This was certainly a bigger and messier job than I had anticipated. Yet looking back on it, I realize this severe demolition was a crucial part of the process.

The last time I experienced a demolition of this extent was when my internal world crumbled at 3:00 a.m. on prom night. Instead of being at the house where everyone was partying, I found myself at the end of a street with my rageful boyfriend, Josh.[*] He yanked my hoodie up, slapped me, and punched my arm—all in a matter of seconds. He then fell to the ground and began to sob while I stood in shock, thinking, *How did I get here?*

We were both wearing black that evening, as he had requested. We camouflaged seamlessly with our surroundings. I thought, *Even if someone came out looking for me, they wouldn't*

---

[*]   "Josh" (pseud.).

be able to see me. I didn't know what to anticipate next. Josh had never raised a hand against me throughout our entire relationship. Had he threatened me before? Sure. *But words are just words,* I thought. *How did I get here? Am I so bad that Josh would hit me? I don't want this to be my story.*

While I tearfully backed away, Josh quickly got up from the ground, grabbed my arm, and muttered, "You'd better not tell anyone what happened." He pulled me back toward the house, loosening his grip only when he saw our friends gathering outside. He flagged down one of the guys, asked him to take me home, and whispered one last threat into my ear before shutting the car door.

Don't say a word.

When I look back on this terrifying high school experience, the answer to that nagging question, *How did I get here?* seems clearer than ever. I didn't just wake up one day and decide to date an abusive and manipulative person. This decision was the culmination of everything I had learned about relationships early on. It made perfect sense that I was attracted to someone like Josh. I couldn't recognize any early signs of abuse, such as narcissistic rage, hypercriticism, and threats. Those behaviors slipped right under my radar—not because Josh was great at hiding them, but because I thought they were normal behaviors.

To me, it was exactly what a relationship—or even love— looked like. I saw it modeled by my family of origin: gaslighting, blaming, hypercriticism, and humiliation. My household had it all. These behaviors were engrained in our family culture, passed down through generations of unresolved trauma and questionable cultural norms. When punishment was given, I was taught that I deserved it, and that it hurt the abuser *more* than it hurt me. In the end, I couldn't discern love from abuse.

Perhaps you've felt the same way at times. Maybe your

circumstances weren't physically violent, but you may have been invalidated or betrayed or found yourself denying your own feelings. Maybe your most important relationships are constantly strained, leading you to ask, *Why does this keep happening to me?* You may have tried to improve yourself to gain approval from others, only to be left feeling like you're never enough. Or, like me, perhaps you struggle with differentiating between love and abuse because your abuser so often danced between the two.

While going about life the best way you knew how, you suddenly found yourself trapped in a demolition that looked totally beyond repair. Your favorite spaces were now destroyed, your safety was suddenly compromised, and your own life no longer seemed livable. *How did I get here? I didn't ask for this story.*

The good news is that if you are asking this question, you are exactly where you need to be. It can be frightening to find yourself in the middle of an unexpected demolition, but you must first dismantle the old if you want to rebuild something new and better. I want you to know that you are not in this scary process alone. I, and many others, have been in the trenches of relational pain and know what it's like to have your hopes and dreams dashed. The hurtful memories can stay with us for decades, but here is the truth: they don't have to have power over us forever. You are not doomed to a miserable life because of your painful past. There is still hope for you, no matter what you did or what has been done to you. You *can* move forward from what happened and experience a beautiful, meaningful, and abundant life. Embrace the demolition, because it is the start of a new life that glorifies God and ignites your soul.

This is why I love using my social platforms to unapologetically share my story of healing with as many people as I can. While I am not a mental health professional, I can bear witness to my own journey of healing and share with you the hope that I have. I wrote *Forever Home* to help you feel fully at home with your own body and experiences, so that you can move beyond *How did I get here?* and build a more joyful and sustainable life. At first it may feel like a teardown, but you can stand firm and trust that it's all part of the ultimate reconstruction of your life.

I don't believe it's a coincidence that you picked up this book. Something in your mind sounded the alarm and told you to inquire further. If you've been wounded by relationships of any sort and aren't sure how to get your life together after the wreckage, let this book be the blueprint for redeeming the remainder of your beautiful story. Most people don't have time to read all the best psychology books or listen to the latest therapeutic podcasts, but I've done the work for you and pulled together a collection of my own transferable wisdom from resources that have helped me most. Ever since I first tasted what healing and wholeness feel like, I've dedicated my life to learning exactly *how* God designed our minds, *why* he designed us this way, and *what* it takes to live the abundant life he intends for us. I can confidently say I am more in sync with my own mind than ever before. My bonds with others continue to grow stronger despite the ups and downs of life. Most of all, I've gained a profound appreciation for Jesus and what he has done for me.

I encourage you to face your real self, even if it's painful at first. Your story is far from over. You have a purpose to fulfill—to live a healthy, abundant, and God-glorifying life. May this book help you embrace your God-given purpose, stop any downward-spiraling thoughts, and break free of harmful scenarios that keep playing over and over in your life. Now is the time to move beyond your challenging past—your demolished house—and build a beautiful "forever home."

"And be sure of this: I am with you always, even to the end of the age."

MATTHEW 28:20

Chapter 1

The Beginning of
My Healing Journey

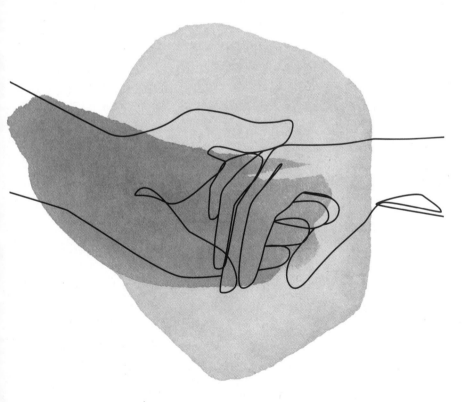

*M*ost of my childhood was spent in transition. My family demolished our mud hut in Vietnam when I was two years old and reconstructed a concrete house in its place. My father's career as an agricultural engineer was thriving at the time, so we could have slowly scaled up our living situation if we had chosen to stay. Instead, we left everything behind and jetted to the United States when I turned four. From there, we migrated from my aunt's tiny bedroom to a humble apartment, to a garage, to a modest ADU (additional dwelling unit), and then, finally, to our first permanent address—a two-bedroom home in the suburbs of El Monte, California, less than 500 feet away from the perpetually packed Interstate 10.

Though our home wasn't in the best location, my parents had big dreams for this house. They were ready to put the past behind them and start fresh in their forever home. I was only twelve years old at the time, but I understood that my parents saw this house as their reward for persevering through war, immigration, and countless other traumas. I was proud of them for accomplishing so much despite being given so little. So with our hearts renewed, we rolled up our sleeves and got to work. I spent hours painting the walls with my father while my mother picked the furniture and managed our bathroom renovation. Day after day, we would work tirelessly to create the cozy home of our dreams. After one full month of renovations, the three of us fell onto our shared mattress and breathed a sigh of relief. We were finally able to rest in our beautiful, stable, and completed home. All was well for the next few weeks, until my father was diagnosed with stage IV stomach cancer.

He died the summer before I entered eighth grade—a mere three months after his diagnosis. His death pulled the rug out from underneath our feet. My mother and I did our best to survive this tremendous loss, but our relationship took a sharp downturn during the spring of my freshman year in high school. As my mother went from being my lifelong best friend to scrutinizing my every move, our mutual trust began to wane. I noticed a lot more contempt from her whenever we talked, and I constantly felt confused and ashamed for falling short of her expectations.

Because of my father's sudden passing, my mother inherited his small business as a taxi driver for the Vietnamese immigrant community. She would get up at 2:00 a.m. to drive her clients to the airport, go home and nap for a few hours, and then get up again at 6:00 a.m. to do more driving. Her unpredictable schedule, coupled with the pressure to pay the mortgage left behind by my late father, drove her to near insanity. Whatever time we had together was filled with so much stress that we would inevitably start bickering. When I entered my sophomore year, she began having weekly nervous breakdowns that took our routine fights to a whole new level. Knives were thrown and computers were broken, and my mother's violent self-harm became a weekly event.

I still remember freezing in panic as she slammed her head against the refrigerator after a small argument. The nervous breakdowns became almost a habit, as over time my mother stopped arguing at all and just ran straight to the kitchen to self-soothe in harmful ways. On days when I had to walk home from school, I had terrifying visions of my mother hanging from the chandelier because she talked about suicide so often. Those awful visions would make me feel so panicked that I would sprint home as quickly as I could. If you were to ask me at that moment what I thought about my future, I would have laughed at your assumption that I had a future at all. Yet God had entirely different plans.

Because of the chaotic environment at home, I tried to seek comfort and stability from my first love—a tall and charming boy named Josh, who was two years older than me. I was fourteen and he was sixteen when we met at a mutual friend's house party. Josh confided in me about his family trauma, and I in him about mine. We snuck out to see each other at night and did all the cheesy things that make for a teen romance.

One day during my marching band practice at the football field, my friend spotted Josh in the bleachers and nudged me to look up. I lowered my clarinet and felt my cheeks flush red. This boy rode his bicycle across the city just to surprise me at band practice. I couldn't remember the last time I had felt that kind of care and adoration. At that point, I would have done anything for Josh because he felt more like family than my own family did. I thought we were deeply and madly in love—until just a year later, when I noticed an eerie shift in his attitude toward me.

During the summer before my junior year, after I came back from a monthlong trip to Vietnam with my mother, Josh became erratic and hostile, saying and doing things that seemed so out of character. He became upset at my most harmless mistakes and raged at me for things like forgetting to put on makeup. It wasn't long before Josh admitted he was getting bored with me and said he felt like he needed to chase after another girl.

"Honestly, you should've seen this coming," he coldly stated. "The word *bored* is in my username. I get bored easily," he said with a shrug.

Once again, I found myself frozen in shock as a once-trusted relationship ended in abandonment.

The kicker was that although Josh wanted the freedom to pursue a new girl, he still wanted control over me. Our relationship became increasingly volatile even while it was on the brink of ending. He kept an eye on my every move through our mutual friends, despite pursuing someone else behind my back. Isn't it ironic how the biggest cheater you know is often the one who is most fearful of being cheated on?

On prom night, Josh spotted one of his friends talking to me, and without asking for any context, he grabbed my wrist and dragged me to the end of the dark street. Josh officially ended our relationship that night with a blow to my left arm before fully committing himself to his new girlfriend, a Christian girl whom he had been chasing during the last six months of our relationship.

At this point, I felt as though I had nowhere to turn. I was unwanted at home and unwanted by my first love. Too afraid to commit suicide, I instead leaned into substance abuse to numb my excruciating loneliness. I started getting trashed at parties every weekend, hoping my life would come to an end without my conscious participation. I dealt with my trauma the only way I knew how—by dissociating.

Dissociation is when you experience a disconnection from yourself—your thoughts, feelings, and sense of identity—in a subconscious effort to cope with whatever is overwhelming you. It can range from scrolling on social media to escape from work stress, to disconnecting from reality altogether in moments of perceived danger. Both people and animals can dissociate as a survival mechanism, as I found out.

The Inescapable Shock

The most pointed example of dissociation I can think of is the "inescapable shock" experiment mentioned in Bessel van der Kolk's *The Body Keeps the Score*. In this cruel and inhumane experiment, researchers administered multiple electric shocks to a group of dogs in cages. They then opened the cage door and shocked the dogs one last time. The group of control dogs who were never electrocuted immediately took off, but the group that was subjected to the shock simply lay there, whimpering and defecating. Van der Kolk reflected, "The mere opportunity to escape does not necessarily make traumatized animals, or people, take the road to freedom. Like [those] dogs, many traumatized people simply give up. Rather than risk experimenting with new options they stay stuck in the fear they know."[1]

Similar to the dogs that were subjected to multiple rounds of electrocution, I was rendered hopeless and helpless by the cyclical trauma I endured. Even if I knew there were options to leave my miserable state of being, I couldn't bring myself to escape the trauma. I was so intimately familiar with my pain that the idea of anything different felt scarier than the pain itself.

Have you ever felt that way? Perhaps you've only recently realized that something in your past was not okay, but at the time, you didn't know any better. You were not equipped to protect yourself from ongoing abuse. You keep replaying the same questions in your head: *How did I let this happen to me? Why can't I just get over this? Am I the only one who feels this way?* These sentiments are often shared by those who have been rendered helpless by their situations.

You are not crazy for feeling the ever-compounding tension of regret, anger, and sorrow because of your painful past. It is okay to grieve the unjust scenarios that never should have happened. If you have trouble moving forward from the anger and grief, however, and find yourself fearing the same scenarios replaying in different relationships, you may be traumatized.

What Is Trauma?

The term *trauma* refers to an emotional response to a distressful experience, usually one that has overwhelmed our ability to cope. Typically, our nervous system only floods our bodies with adrenaline when it detects danger, and then it goes back to normal when the danger goes away. However, if we are unable to cope with the distress, the effects of our fear can be lodged inside our bodies and resurface whenever we sense a similar threat. This is what is known as a "trigger." Chronic exposure to situations that render us fearful and helpless can change our brain chemistry to be on a continual high-alert mode. Our nervous system becomes overly sensitive and causes us to react to triggers in disproportionate ways.

Unfortunately, if our bodies are stuck in survival mode and have a higher baseline of anxiety, we can suffer from insomnia, depression, irritation, and feelings of helplessness, as well as a plethora of other negative impacts.[2] Each person responds to trauma differently, depending on the type of trauma we endured, the age at which we experienced the trauma, and a combination of nature and nurture (our genetic dispositions and how we were raised).[3] Some people get violently triggered by their trauma, while others shut down.

When I was in high school, my body knew I couldn't fight back against the people who hurt me, so in a subconscious effort to survive, I engaged in countless dissociative activities. Believe it or not, even self-destructive tendencies are the body's vain efforts to protect itself.

Like the dogs in the inescapable shock experiment, I continued to self-sabotage to numb the pain. I even had moments when I thought I would shut down completely.

My Escape

One Saturday night, I was so intoxicated at a house party that I lost all sense of where I was and couldn't even sense the temperature around me. Toward the end of the party, I remember stumbling into the back seat of a stranger's car. The car quickly filled up with my friends, all of whom were just as intoxicated as I was. The driver turned up the techno music and took off into the night. I was suddenly overwhelmed by the emptiness in my life and began sobbing in the back seat. The music blasted right over me as though I had no voice at all.

Then a very clear, poignant thought entered my mind: *Nobody truly loves you.* I had never felt more terrified of loneliness than at that very moment. I cried harder for help, in much the same way as an infant wailing. Miraculously, someone responded to my cries.

In my mind's eye, I saw the painting of Jesus that my mother had hung in my childhood home. I had never really thought about that altar before because I didn't share my mother's Catholic faith. Although I was forced to take catechism classes as a child, I was too young to understand the religious teachings and sermons— especially because they were in formal Vietnamese, of which I had only a very elementary grasp.[4] I stopped attending my Catholic church altogether when my relationship with my mother fell apart and adopted the agnostic worldview. Yet when I was in my darkest place, I felt that Jesus had met me through that vision.

My cries were calmed when I saw this painting in my mind. I then noticed a feeling of comfort washing over me, from the top of my head down to my shoulders, cloaking my arms and waist, and continuing all the way down to my toes. It felt like a warm, all-encompassing, full-body hug. I was swaddled in it for what felt like the longest, most soothing minute of my life. I had never experienced that kind of comfort before.

After that divine hug was lifted, I completely snapped out of my intoxicated mess and asked the driver to take me home. That following school day, I approached the only Christian friend I knew and told her about my experience in that car. Her eyes lit up when I mentioned the painting of Jesus, and she invited me to her family's church to learn more about him. It was nothing short of an act of grace that I was led to this specific friend, who shouldered my story without judgment and kindly invited me into her spiritual home.

That Sunday, I attended my very first Protestant church service, heard the gospel preached in a way I could understand for the first time, and accepted Christ as my Lord and Savior. To meet Jesus felt like I was given a second chance at life. He empowered me to break out of my self-sabotaging cage and start building a life that felt more like a sanctuary than a sinkhole. This experience marked the beginning of my journey back to wholeness.

No Longer Enslaved to Fear

Sometimes God allows us to reach our lowest point so we can finally look up toward him. I had no intentions of turning to religion for help, let alone becoming a devout Christian. Yet when I was at my lowest point, Jesus heard my agonizing cries and came to my rescue. He was attuned to my needs and comforted me when I was at my most difficult to console. His compassion gave me hope and allowed me to live in true freedom.

Jesus essentially led me away from learned helplessness and victimhood, just like what the researchers had to do with the dogs in the experiment. Bessel van der Kolk explained, "The only way to teach traumatized dogs to get off the electric grids when the doors were open was to repeatedly drag them out of their cages so they could physically experience how they could get away."[5] And that was exactly what happened when I encountered Jesus in the back seat of that car. I had a visceral experience of freedom—the comforting, spiritual hug—that opened my mind to the possibility of healing. Without that life-changing encounter with Jesus, I wouldn't have known how to break the cycle of trauma in my life. I would have behaved just like the helpless dogs, whimpering in my own fear while staring at a cage door that was swinging wide open.

Although my life wasn't instantly fixed after I came to believe in Jesus, my faith in him helped me endure through the heartbreaks that ensued. My redeeming relationship with Jesus allowed me to reflect on past events in a healthier way and make sense of the difficult relationships that pained me. I slowly discovered what it meant to feel worthy and cared for rather than worthless and burdensome. I learned that my worth was not based on what my mother thought about me or the way Josh had treated me, but that I had intrinsic worth because God had created me out of his great love. I was created by love and for love—what a thought!

As I journeyed with Jesus through the difficult seasons thereafter, I became increasingly more secure in my relationship with him, myself, and others. Perhaps this is what healing is all about, at least on this side of heaven. A life with Jesus doesn't mean a trouble-free path, but one filled with obstacles that I can bravely overcome without giving in to fear.

My encounter with Jesus marked the start of a new journey toward building a solid foundation of love. I learned so many beautiful lessons along the way about humanity and healing that I'm eager to share with you. I'm not here to diagnose you, but rather to disrupt the dysfunctional norm of what you're experiencing and help you find a life-giving pathway forward. I pray that this will be the beginning of your healing journey too. May the God of compassion meet you right here and now and cover you with his reassuring embrace. In Jesus' name. Amen.

"Come to me, all you who are weary and burdened, and I will give you rest."

MATTHEW 11:28 NIV

Foundation

The only love that won't disappoint you is one that can't change, that can't be lost, that is not based on the ups and downs of life or of how well you live. It is something that not even death can take away from you. God's love is the only thing like that.

Timothy Keller, *Walking with God through Pain and Suffering*

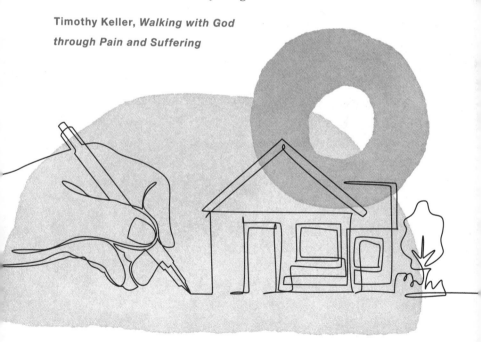

I remember the exact moment when all of my separate experiences of pain and suffering felt like they had merged into one massive boulder atop my shoulders. The sadness of losing my father, the resentfulness of bearing the brunt of my mother's breakdowns, and the heartache of being abused by my first love overwhelmed me to the core. My problems seemed insurmountable, and every day felt like a darkness I couldn't overcome. I was slowly crumbling under this enormous weight while the people around me were frantic about what to do. The weight I was carrying seemed to scare everyone away—even those who were closest to me. Some would tread lightly toward me to offer consolation, only to run for the hills as soon as they caught a glimpse of my immense trauma. Others thought I was just too weak, convinced that they could do a much better job of handling this trauma if it were theirs. Still, the darkest thought of all while losing control of my life was that I was destined to go through it all alone.

If there's one thing the enemy loves to do, it is to make us feel isolated in our suffering. In our isolation, he is free to consume our thoughts, poison our joys, and destroy our hopes for the future. Yet he lives in constant fear that one day we'll realize the truth: that even in our darkest moments of suffering, Jesus is and always has been enduring it alongside us. Indeed, we were never truly alone. The reason we haven't completely crumbled is because Jesus has been continuously upholding us and securing our footing. What he yearns for is to give us a solid foundation, one that is built on his unchanging and unconditional love for us.

Here is the truth: Jesus loves you. He has a love for you that is unlike any other love you have ever known. He loves you in your weakness, and he loves you in your trauma. He loves you so fiercely that he laid down his life for you. Your problems are not too big for him to step into and address. He isn't deterred by your brokenness. Jesus values you, has hopes for you, and endures with you.

It's time to build a new foundation on the love of Jesus. Forget the foundations of the past—none of them will be able to sustain the new "house" you will build. God intends for your life to be like a sturdy, peaceful, and safe house, and such a house requires a new, solid foundation that will not shift when the storms of life hit. As Timothy Keller reminds us, God's love is the only foundation like that.

Chapter 2
You Are Loved

*We are not necessarily doubting that God
will do the best for us: we are wondering
how painful the best will turn out to be.*

C. S. Lewis, "Letter to Father
Peter Bide," April 29, 1959

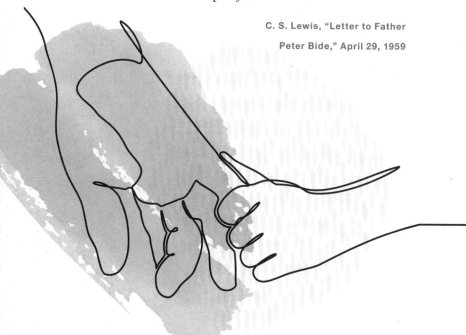

*E*stablishing a firm foundation is critical to any home-building project, especially if we are rebuilding our lives after our traumatic experiences. As I write this book, I'm in the process of renovating my very first home, so the topic of fortifying a foundation is fresh in my mind. One of the first things my structural engineer had to do was inspect the foundation to evaluate whether it could withstand the new tensions and weight being placed on it. A good foundation should last several lifetimes.

In the Bible, Jesus uses the analogy of building a good foundation to distinguish between wise and foolish builders. "Anyone who listens to my teaching and follows it is wise, like a person who builds a house on solid rock," said Jesus. "Though the rain comes in torrents and the floodwaters rise and the winds beat against that house, it won't collapse because it is built on bedrock" (Matthew 7:24–25).

We can have the most wonderful finishes and fixtures, so to speak, but if the foundation is weak, everything will come crumbling down once the storms of life come. As you'll soon discover, the primary job of our caretakers is to provide this bedrock of love and safety for us when we are born. Without this foundation of love, we will be less resilient in response to the effects of trauma, which may maintain a foothold on our reactions and relationships. Unfortunately, not everyone has grown up with consistent parenting—parenting that emulates the unchanging and unconditional love of God. As a consequence, many of us developed insecure attachment styles that have left us vulnerable to the storms of life. If we do not feel inherently loved in our current situations, we cannot feel safe and begin to heal. This notion is echoed by psychologists Henry Cloud and John Townsend in their book *Our Mothers, Ourselves*:

> We must be nurtured before we can begin to think and use language. This is why babies begin talking in the second year of life, after they have received a lot of nurture. In this way, thinking rests on a bedrock of safety and security so that it is relatively unhampered by the need for love. . . . This is why some efforts at positive thinking fail. The problem is not with the thinking, but with the lack of love underneath. Insecure people think insecure thoughts.[1]

Cloud and Townsend emphasize the importance of love as the bedrock for safety, and safety as the bedrock for positive thinking. We cannot force ourselves to become positive thinkers if we inherently feel unloved and unsafe. After all, children need to receive a lot of care and nurture from their caregivers in order to develop optimally.[2] Without a secure foundation of love, children can experience all sorts of developmental problems and medical conditions later in life. Neglect, parental inconsistency, and lack

You can build a new house on a *secure foundation* of God's love that will last a *lifetime.*

of affection can leave deep-seated scars that limit our potential and erode our happiness over time.[3] Studies have shown that the early wounds of life can fester into chronic inflammation, opening the door to a host of age-related illnesses.[4] From heart disease to cancer, inflammation caused by an overactive nervous system can cast a long shadow over both our present and our future. Simply put, when love is inconsistent or absent, the soul and the body suffer in ways we never could have imagined.

But here is the good news: although you did not have control over how you were raised, you are not doomed to the sad destiny of someone without love. You *are* loved. Because of this unending love, you can, in fact, build a new house on a secure

ANXIOUS	AVOIDANT
• Having difficulty trusting others	• Having trouble expressing or recognizing emotions
• Possessing a low self-worth	• Disliking physical affection and intimacy
• Fearing abandonment	• Feeling easily suffocated by a partner's needs
• Continually longing for intimacy	• Rejecting emotional support from others
• Being overly dependent in relationships	• Fearing emotional intimacy, yet still desiring it
• Having a constant need for reassurance	• Valuing personal independence more than closeness with others
• Being highly sensitive to a partner's behavior and mood	• Being emotionally detached during times of stress
• Being impulsive and unpredictable	• Exhibiting a stoic demeanor in intense emotional situations
• Being easily emotional	• Preferring to handle things alone rather than relying on a partner

foundation of God's love that will last a lifetime. As we gear up to do this, let's first talk about attachment styles.

Attachment Theory

I learned about attachment theory when I came across the works of the British psychologist John Bowlby, who described attachment as the "lasting psychological connectedness between human beings."[5] Four attachment styles have been identified: anxious, avoidant, disorganized, and secure. The table below helps you to identify with one or more styles. You can put a checkmark next to the points that are true for you:[6]

DISORGANIZED	SECURE
• Having a mixture of anxious and avoidant attachment styles	• Being confident
• Having chaotic, unpredictable, or intense relationship patterns and behaviors	• Being empathetic
• Fearing rejection and having difficulty in trusting others, leading to isolation	• Possessing strong self-validation and self-awareness
• Craving intimacy while also pushing others away	• Being balanced in giving and receiving in relationships
• Possessing a negative self-image and low self-worth	• Being responsive, but typically nonreactive
• Feeling shameful and unworthy of love	• Being able to navigate conflicts in a healthy manner
• Aggression or fear toward caregivers and partners	• Enjoying healthy social connections
• Possessing a deep-seated sense of inadequacy and worthlessness	• Being able to trust and feeling trusted in relationships
	• Being open to vulnerability and intimacy
	• Respecting personal needs and boundaries while maintaining healthy relationships

⚡ *Anxious Attachment*

If you have an anxious attachment style, you may fear abandonment or rejection, need constant reassurance in relationships, or be prone to becoming emotionally dysregulated, which means you may have trouble managing and controlling your emotions. Those who struggle with emotional dysregulation may find it difficult to identify their emotions and communicate them effectively, which can lead to further frustration. Sometimes their emotions may feel so intense and overwhelming that they spill out in ways that don't match the situation. It's like a firework going off in a library— startling, out of place, and potentially damaging.

I once identified most with the anxious attachment style. After my trauma with Josh, it was like a switch went off in my brain, and I became deeply insecure in all of my close relationships. My hypersensitivity to abandonment skyrocketed, causing my first anxiety attack in college after what had felt like a moment of abandonment by someone I loved. I was extremely distrustful of people and paranoid of betrayal. The closer I got to someone, the less I trusted them. My heightened baseline of anxiety made me feel triggered by even the smallest offenses, so I often found it difficult to control my emotions in close relationships.

Although research is inconclusive about what causes someone to be anxiously attached, the most likely contributing factor is inconsistent and misattuned parenting. Misattunement refers to a caregiver's failure to respond appropriately to a child's emotional needs. This can manifest in a variety of ways, such as ignoring a child's distress, being inconsistent with affection and attention, or dismissing a child's emotions altogether. When caregivers don't provide consistent or attuned responses, a child's brain can get overwhelmed with harmful stress hormones, which puts the child at a greater risk of developing anxiety disorders in the future.[7]

After I learned about the anxious attachment style, my

mother's stories about how I was a difficult baby started to make sense. She often told our neighbors and relatives that it was hard to soothe me as an infant. I would scream and cry so intensely that my feet would bleed from the friction of rubbing them together. I was, by all accounts, an anxious baby.

To soothe their upset child, my well-meaning but undereducated parents would try everything from superstitious remedies to misdiagnosing me with all sorts of maladies they had learned from old wives' tales. Nothing worked, of course, because their care was misattuned. Out of their deep distress of being unable to soothe their baby, my parents eventually gave up and allowed me to "cry it out." Years later, I would find myself in the same spot as in infancy—crying and hyperventilating at the thought of being misunderstood and abandoned.

Avoidant Attachment

If you have an avoidant attachment style, you may also fear abandonment or rejection, cope by becoming detached and distanced, or avoid relational conflict by withdrawing. I have a friend named Kent* who has a textbook avoidant attachment style. I could tell that Kent loved his family because he was a faithful provider and a loyal husband, but as I interviewed him for this book, he shared that he often found it difficult to give his wife the connection and empathy she needed. He expressed that when their marriage turned sour due to the lack of a deeper connection, he withdrew further into his work and spent days in the dissociative retreat of his office. Kent avoided all difficult conversations and often left his wife wanting more from their interactions.

His dismissive-avoidant attachment style ran its course in his other relationships as well. Though he was generally outgoing and extroverted, he reportedly consistently had trouble

---

* "Kent" (pseud.).

creating deep bonds with others. He had many different circles of friends, but all were characterized by either weak ties or shallow connections. Kent shared that this was because he was easily overwhelmed by others' emotional needs and often found their problems burdensome. He was never taught how to properly make sense of his own feelings, let alone help someone else work through their emotional conflicts. I recalled how it had taken years of my consistent friendship before he felt comfortable enough to move past the polite small talk and share with me more of his honest struggles.

As one may expect, an avoidant attachment style can develop due to emotionally unavailable parenting. Parents or caregivers who disregard the child's emotional needs and limit the showing of affection can set the child up to disregard both their own needs and the needs of others. The child does not inherit the necessary social-emotional tools—such as empathy, affection, and relationship management—to establish and maintain deep bonds.

Kent shared that when he was in primary school, he encountered a bully on a field trip who demanded that he kneel down and tie the bully's shoes. Kent's mother, a chaperone that day, saw this incident unfold as she stepped out of the school bus. She waited and observed in silence. Afterward, Kent ran to her for comfort and protection, but she appeared visibly upset and reprimanded him for not standing up for himself. She then disregarded both Kent and the bully and joined the other chaperones as though nothing had happened.

Outside of providing for Kent's basic needs, his parents failed to empathize with him and validate his emotional experiences. Kent expressed that he and his siblings never went to bed hungry, but they also never got to experience affirming protection, empathy, or validation from their parents. Like clockwork, he would repeat this same cycle of dismissiveness and irritation when his wife would come to him for empathy. "It's not that I didn't love her, because I did," he said. "It's just that I couldn't give what I didn't have. But I'm learning that it doesn't have to be this way." He generously granted me permission to share his story in detail in the hope that it would help others connect the dots in their own lives.

Disorganized Attachment

If you have a disorganized attachment style, you may be fearful in relationships, display erratic behavior under relational stress, or be prone to emotional dysregulation. The disorganized attachment style is a blend between the anxious and avoidant attachment styles, giving it the moniker "the anxious-avoidant attachment style." Like anxiously attached persons, disorganized-attached individuals may be deeply insecure in their relationships and need constant reassurance. However, because they also have an avoidant attachment style, they may be less confrontational about their internal conflicts than the anxiously attached. Instead, they may live in quiet expectation of eventual rejection or disappointment. Their unresolved anxiety and lack of communication may also play a part in self-sabotaging their relationships.

Years ago, I became good friends with a purehearted and enthusiastic woman named Grace.** Grace told me she prided herself on being a good helper and listener, and I can attest that she was. I noticed that because Grace was so quick to help her friends at the drop of a hat, she became close friends with everyone she met. People loved Grace because she was always available to help them resolve their relationship problems, accompany them on errands, and even do their chores. The problem was, of course, that Grace did not always have the emotional capacity or even the desire to do those things. She just

---

** "Grace" (pseud.).

couldn't set boundaries because of her need to please the people she loved.

There were also moments in her friendships that deeply bothered her, but she didn't know how to express her needs directly. Eventually, Grace hid from most of her friends. She withdrew from her community, which she once loved fervently, and isolated herself for months. During a brief moment when Grace emerged from her isolation, she told me her true thoughts about each person she had once helped. It was clear that Grace had many valid feelings she didn't know how to express that had turned into anxious resentfulness. Grace found herself in a constant cycle of becoming overly committed, burning out, and isolating from her formerly close friends.

Like many people with a disorganized attachment style, Grace grew up with unpredictable and inconsistent parenting. She saw her parents carefully structure her brother's academic career and provide for his basic needs, such as giving him lunch money each day, while she received much less attention and care. She didn't always receive lunch money and didn't get nearly as much academic coaching as her brother—and on top of the neglect, she had to constantly be the mediator in her parents' fights. Instead of being consistently cared for, Grace found herself parenting her own caretakers. It is no wonder that years later, Grace would still be striving to earn the love and care she desperately needed by overcommitting her time and attention to others, only to burn out and become discouraged when she found herself, yet again, in lack.

 ### *Secure Attachment*

If you have a secure attachment style, you are able to form positive, lasting, and loving relationships with others. A person who is securely attached has the emotional infrastructure to trust people and establish emotional intimacy while maintaining healthy boundaries. They do not panic or get overly anxious when their loved ones need time and space apart. When friends disappoint them, they do not quickly resort to all-or-nothing thinking or instinctively cope by withdrawing. A securely attached person knows how to give and receive love, depend on others without losing their independence, and forgive others while maintaining their sense of boundaries.

There are tangible benefits to becoming a securely attached person. Research shows that securely attached individuals experience more joy, feel better about themselves, reflect on their thoughts and emotions more accurately, and have more effective coping strategies compared to those with insecure attachment styles.[8] This is why the goal of this chapter is to inspire and guide you toward becoming a deeply secure person whose foundation rests firmly on the love of God. When we anchor ourselves in God's unshakable love, we have a sturdy foundation for a fulfilling and resilient life.

The more I study the secure attachment style, the more I'm reminded of the character of Jesus. Though being of equal standing with God, Jesus lowered himself to be born into a dirty manger and lead a humble life for thirty years. In Jesus' thirtieth year, he began his ministry by recruiting those coming from lowly backgrounds to be the foundation of his legacy. He enlisted a tax collector, a thief, a band of fishermen, and five other men of unimpressive social standing as his closest friends. Jesus trusted these twelve disciples and they trusted him (for the most part). Even when he found out that one of them would betray him, instead of erupting in a fit of rage and abandoning all of his other disciples, Jesus proceeded to draw *closer* to them by breaking bread with them over one last, intimate supper.

Jesus also brought his internal conflicts to the Father at the Mount of Olives, where he knelt down and earnestly prayed, "Father, if you are willing, take this cup from me; yet not my will, but yours be done" (Luke 22:42 NIV). Despite Jesus' agonizing torment, he surrendered his situation to God and accepted the painful road that lay before him as a part of God's greater plan for humanity. This act of surrender is the ultimate display of his secure attachment to God the Father.

The Bible states that after an angel appeared to Jesus to strengthen him, Jesus was still in anguish and his sweat was "like drops of blood falling to the ground" (Luke 22:44 NIV). This tells us that being securely attached doesn't mean we will be immune to the anguishes of the human experience. We can feel the deepest sorrow and still choose to believe that God is going to work everything out for the greater good. Jesus trusted his heavenly Father on both the good and bad days. He always prayed to God as a first response rather than a last resort. His secure attachment to the Father gave him the mental and spiritual fortitude to endure all kinds of harrowing temptations and trials.

As shown through Jesus' example, a secure attachment style comes from having a healthy bond with parents who are consistent and responsive to the child's needs. When parents are self-controlled and attuned to their child's needs, the child feels safe, seen, comforted, valued, and confident.

Children who are securely attached to their parents also feel safe to explore, as we can see from the brief glimpse into Jesus' childhood in the gospel of Luke. At age twelve, Jesus went on a customary trip with his earthly family to Jerusalem for the Passover festival. When the festival ended, his parents and their company made their way back home, but Jesus stayed in Jerusalem to sit among the religious teachers at the temple, "listening to them and asking them questions" (Luke 2:46 NIV). Though his curiosity caused his parents anxiety as they frantically searched for him, his desire to learn and explore was age-appropriate. Jesus then followed them back to Nazareth and "was obedient to them" (2:51 NIV). He demonstrated his ability to trust others and be trusted at a young age, revealing his secure attachment to both his earthly parents and his heavenly Father. It is no surprise that he steadily "grew in wisdom and stature, and in favor with God and man" (2:52 NIV).

The Perfect Father

Jesus' attachment to God the Father is as perfectly secure as it can get because he *is* one with the Father, but here is the good news: believers have the same access to our heavenly Father that Jesus does. After all, this is why Jesus took our sins on himself—so that everyone who believes can experience reconciliation with our heavenly Father. When we place our faith in Jesus, not only are we free from the burdens of our own sins, but we also gain the peace and safety we need to heal from the sins of others.

Belief in Jesus allows us to have access to the most attuned, loving, and consistent Father there is—the Creator of the

Belief in Jesus allows us to have access to the most attuned, loving, and consistent *Father* there is.

universe himself. Because Jesus died for us and covered us with his redeeming love, our relationship with the Father has been restored. We can come boldly to him for help, comfort, and guidance during every part of our day, and we can rest in the security that he will show up for us each time (Joshua 1:9; Isaiah 41:10; Matthew 28:20).

Believe, Belong, Become

If you identified strongly with one of the insecure attachment styles but are afraid you can't make a change, please take heart. Not only is it possible for you to earn security in adulthood; you have access to a tried-and-true formula to help improve the way you give and receive love. By rebuilding a foundation of security and love, you are laying the groundwork for a life that is both enjoyable to you and edifying to everyone around you. It is time to restore your sense of stability by exchanging the confusion of *How did I get here?* for the confidence of *I'm exactly where I want to be.*

In a 2019 study, twenty individuals who had a history of insecure attachment were put through a series of therapeutic interactions to see if they could develop secure attachment in their adulthood.[9] All twenty people benefited from the experiment and showed the ability to earn secure attachments, with many choosing to become surrogate attachment figures or mentors to someone else at the end of the research. This is the beautiful redemption that can come after the messy demolition. Once you clear out the clutter, you can reconstruct a foundation that can fully support the weight of your forever home.

Through the many intentional and positive interactions between the research participants and their clinicians, the researchers discovered three main conditions in which insecure adults can "earn" security:

1. **Believe:** believing in your inherent worthiness.
2. **Belong:** having a network of supportive and meaningful relationships.
3. **Become:** becoming a secure person in the way you think about yourself and others.

Believing You Are Worthy

Each research participant was matched with a mental health clinician who served as their surrogate attachment figure and mentor. The clinicians earned the participants' trust by providing a consistent, positive experience each time they engaged in talk therapy. As a result of receiving this type of positive mentorship, the participants wanted to change the way they gave and received love. This single positive relationship with their clinicians instilled hope that they were worthy of healing and capable of having secure relationships.

This shows that if we want to establish a stronger foundation that is based on God's love, we first must have at least one surrogate attachment figure who can help us be intentional about making peace with our past and redefining our worth. They must make us feel as though we are inherently worthy, not because of any external accomplishments or efforts, but because of who we are. In other words, our surrogate attachment figure must help us discover our God-given worth. Then we will have the necessary support to make real, lasting changes to our attachment style.

Brilliantly enough, this is exactly what a relationship with Jesus can do for many people who struggle with an insecure attachment style. A meaningful encounter with Jesus gives people the glimmer of hope that healing is possible. No matter who you choose as your mentor or attachment figure, having a firm relationship with Jesus will only help you in your journey of healing. He will always be available to guide and comfort you when you need him most, moving you toward a deeper connection with him and others.

Without experiencing a taste of relational security first, it is extremely difficult and unlikely for a person to positively change the way they experience love. This gives a new meaning to the phrase *born again* for Christians who come to know Christ later in life. The old insecure habits of relating to others pass away, and the new child of God emerges. The born-again Christian now has access to a secure relationship with God that empowers them to stay hopeful and intentional as they learn how to relate to others in healthier ways.

Belonging in a Community

In addition to cultivating a close relationship with Jesus, we also need to be firmly rooted in meaningful relationships with others. We are social beings at our core, with every element of our makeup designed to be deeply integrated with the community around us. You can begin making these meaningful and supportive bonds in support groups, churches, and anywhere else that can help you create relationships that are sensitive to the impact of trauma on your life. To make this process easier, I've compiled a list of support groups and helpful organizations in the back of the book. I hope these recommendations help you find a community near you that can bear witness to your story and accept you wholeheartedly.

Alcoholics Anonymous (AA) is a program I recommend. I had a close friend whose father was a high-functioning alcoholic. He was a single father of four who paid the bills on time and put food on the table for his children. His children knew him to be a wonderful father. However, his emotional life was in shambles. His workday couldn't begin until he had made his way to the local bar and downed a few shots of liquor. He couldn't bear being sober for too long because of the emotional pain he felt. Eventually, the alcohol manifested in serious health issues, and he checked himself into rehab. He joined an AA group immediately after he was discharged. His life took a drastic turn for the better with the support of his fellow AA members.

Members of AA are given tools—mentors, spiritual belief, accountability groups, and so forth—to help them endure through some of the toughest moments of addiction. During moments of intense withdrawal symptoms, good habits on their own are not enough to help members through their dark nights of the soul. Only the guidance of a surrogate attachment figure, the belief in a higher power, and the constancy of a support group can help someone endure through those gut-wrenching moments.

You, too, have the capacity to change your thought patterns and the quality of your life with the right support and guidance. You are not doomed to defeat because of things that were outside of your control, such as your early upbringing or the trauma you witnessed. You are on a journey of healing, and the right relationships can catapult you toward the breakthrough you've been waiting for.

Becoming the Person You're Meant to Be

According to research, feeling a sense of belonging and having a belief system in place are foundational to making internal shifts that lead to secure attachment, such as developing a securely attached perspective.[10] Securely attached individuals have a clearer sense of self-worth and purpose, allowing them to feel at ease in the absence of danger and take action when necessary. Their regulated nervous systems contribute to their ability to maintain inner peace and engage with the world. Compared to those with insecure attachment, they have a stronger sense of identity and direction in life.

Lasting positive change requires more than just external modifications. To achieve lasting transformation, people must undergo deep internal changes at the cognitive, emotional, and spiritual levels. In the context of the 2019 research sample group, the participants had to redefine their identity and self-worth, ultimately letting go of the victim mindset that held them back.[11] Our past does not have to define our present or future. While the scars of our childhood and past experiences may remain, they do not have to dictate the trajectory of our lives. We can break free from negative patterns and beliefs by fostering healthy and supportive relationships and internalizing the truth that we are inherently valuable and worthy, regardless of what others may have said or done to us. With the right mindset and support, we can overcome the victim mentality and go down a more empowering and fulfilling path.

A Testament of Love

My life is a living proof that even the most entrenched wounds can be transformed into hope and resilience. For most of my adult years, I grappled with relationship anxiety, a by-product of the deficient nurturing I received in childhood and the traumatic events I endured in my adolescence. It was easy to succumb to victimhood and allow my past to define my present. But Jesus intervened and showed me a path forward. I discovered that hope and healing were possible through the love and support of God, my close circle of friends, and my therapist. With perseverance and the support of my loved ones, I broke free from the shackles of my past and discovered the joy of living a life unencumbered by anxiety and self-doubt.

If you're searching for a way to earn security and healing

as an adult, begin by opening your heart to Jesus. It's not about mustering willpower or feigning optimism, but rather about surrendering your pain and thought distortions to a higher power. When you ask for divine help, Jesus will meet you where you are and help you overcome the lies that are keeping you trapped.

Even if you decide to trust God, a part of you may fear the pain of the journey. It's okay to feel hesitant about surrendering your life to Jesus, especially if you've been betrayed before. People you've trusted and cared for may have let you down in the past, leaving you abandoned when you needed them the most. The fear of being hurt again is real. But remember, there is power in choosing to trust despite your fears. With Jesus, you have the opportunity to experience a love that never fails, a peace that exceeds all understanding, and a hope that anchors your soul. Take the risk and watch as he transforms your pain into purpose.

The kind of love that God has for us is summed up in a well-known passage—1 Corinthians 13:4–7 (NIV):

> Love is patient, love is kind. It does not envy, it does not boast, it is not proud. It does not dishonor others, it is not self-seeking, it is not easily angered, it keeps no record of wrongs. Love does not delight in evil but rejoices with the truth. It always protects, always trusts, always hopes, always perseveres.

This is the unconditional love that we can find in Jesus himself. Jesus doesn't make idle promises to win us over; he demonstrated his love by dying on our behalf. His sacrifice on the cross is a reminder of his unwavering devotion to us. Unlike the flawed people in our lives, Jesus is not just well-meaning; he always follows through on his promises. His love for us is real and enduring, and he has proven it time and time again.

My goal is to show you how to experience this securely attached love with God, yourself, and others so that you can break free from the chains of your past. I pray that God meets you where you are and gives you a taste of the boundless freedom that comes with a life of healing and wholeness. In Jesus' name. Amen.

Praise be to God,
who has not rejected my prayer
or withheld his love from me!

PSALM 66:20 NIV

Just for You

Take a deep breath and allow yourself to process all that you've learned. These reflection questions will guide you on your faith journey and help you do a deep dive into your thoughts and emotions. You can use them as journaling prompts or as discussion questions with your small group. Remember, you're not alone on this journey, and there's no need to rush. Take your time, and allow God to reveal his wisdom at every turn.

1. Out of the four attachment styles, which one do you identify with the most?
2. How does it make you feel to know you can change your attachment style?
3. Out of the three main ways to earn security (believing in your worth, belonging in your tribe, and becoming who you are meant to be), which step do you want to take in this season?

Let's Pray Together

Dear heavenly Father, I ask for your comfort and guidance today. Please remind me of all the ways you love me so deeply, so I can live from a place of true security. I want to know what it's like to have your love as the solid foundation of my life. Please continue to walk with me as I unearth the pains of my past, and show me how to live in true freedom and abundance. In Jesus' name. Amen.

Chapter 3

Believing You Are Worthy

In this season God intends to give us an unshakable identity in Him, that no amount of adoration nor rejection can alter.

Alicia Britt Chole, *Anonymous: Jesus' Hidden Years . . . and Yours*

*A*s I stepped through the doors of the church I had faithfully attended since 2018, I was greeted with a pleasant surprise. The red carpet was rolled out and the much-loved popcorn machine was sitting front and center. We were beginning a new series titled "At the Movies," in which the preachers would dissect blockbusters that echo biblical stories. The movie for that Sunday's sermon was *Toy Story 4.*

Our senior pastor, Pastor Tom, jokingly opened with the admonition, "Don't you dare call this a kids' movie!" I looked over at my husband, who seemed awkwardly amused. Pastor Tom continued, "The greatest stories ever told—whether on the silver screen or in the pages of a book—are but dim reflections of what we find in Scripture." He caught my attention with that line, but the truth was that I felt like it would be a stretch to compare *Toy Story 4* with anything relevant to the Bible. Still, I decided to give him a chance.

If you haven't seen *Toy Story 4* or need a refresher, the story begins with a five-year-old girl named Bonnie. Bonnie was beyond nervous during her first day of kindergarten, so she created a makeshift toy using random craft items, like a spork, pipe cleaners, and some googly eyes. Despite its hodgepodge appearance, this wonky little fork figure became Bonnie's first friend. She lovingly wrote her name on his popsicle-stick feet and named him Forky.

After his lighthearted recap, Pastor Tom said, "Do you see what's happening? Forky was created from random pieces of trash—a spork, a broken popsicle stick, a little bit of pipe cleaner—all so much more than the sum of its parts. Somehow this collection is actually loved and brought to life. Does this narrative sound familiar in any way?" I saw where he was going and braced myself for a potential sermon about how we as God's people are actually trash.

He continued, "In Genesis 2, it says, 'Then the LORD God formed man from the dust of the ground and breathed into his nostrils the breath of life, and the man became a living being'" (Genesis 2:7 NIV).

I winced. There was only one connection to make from all of this.

"Friends, let's not gloss over this," he said. "The Creator literally formed man—all of humanity—from the dust of the ground. *Worthless, meaningless dust.* What do you do with dust? You try to *get rid* of dust. Dust, at best, is composed of after-thought particles. At worst, it is *microscopic waste.*"

At this point, I was having flashbacks of the times I had heard other Christians preach messages of shame and worthless-ness. I remembered hearing about how even my good deeds were like filthy rags in the eyes of the Lord—that nothing I could ever do would please him or impress him because I am, at my core, just *not good enough.*

Don't get me wrong. I understand the idea behind it—that we can't earn our salvation by our good deeds or impress God with how "good" we are. But I'm not convinced that this way of preaching does justice to the heart of God. He is a Father, after all, so what kind of good Father would take pleasure in hear-ing his children be told that they are worthless and not good enough? This situation seemed to me like a form of spiritual abuse or, at the very least, emotional harm. We as God's people are already bombarded with shame-activating messages like these on billboards and in advertisements, and in movies and music alike. We are told we should be ashamed of how we look and who we are so that companies can exploit our insecurities and control our spending habits. Was it the same for the church? After all, feeling ashamed doesn't make us want to draw closer to God; rather, it makes us want to hide under a rock. I believe this is one of the most diabolical ways the enemy has defiled our sense of connection with our Creator. He spews out lies such as:

- You're not good enough.
- You're worthless.
- You're nothing but a meaningless clump of cells.
- You're unloved.
- You're shameful.

And regretfully, some of these lies are echoed repeatedly by none other than God's own people and through traumatic experiences that leave us questioning ourselves and our sanity. Perhaps you haven't heard the message of worthlessness preached in a church, but you've heard it taught elsewhere—in your classrooms, friend groups, or even your own home. Hearing it again from a pulpit may be the twisted kind of confirmation that the enemy loves to exploit.

The opening of his sermon certainly made me anxious. Nonetheless, Pastor Tom continued, "Yet the God of the universe actually gathered dust . . ."

Pastor Tom bent down on one knee and made a gathering motion with his hands.

"And from this dust . . ."

The pastor made a *fwhoosh* blowing sound.

"He breathes intelligence."

Fwooosh.

"He breathes passions and emotions."

Fwooosh.

"Spirit and soul."

Then he cupped both of his hands and said, "God breathed the breath of life into the dust of the ground, and it became a living *image bearer* of himself."

The anxious stirring of my soul fell quiet. This wasn't the sermon I had feared after all. Pastor Tom was emphasizing the worthlessness of the dust to juxtapose it with the Creator's love for his creation. To us, the dust may seem worthless—something to get rid of—but to God, it was the crafting material he used to lovingly create image bearers of himself. The whole was truly greater than the sum of its parts. This was the perfect illustration of how we were *given worth* by our Creator.

Pastor Tom continued, "By the way, did you catch the subtlety at the very end of the clip there? Did you notice that on the bottom of Forky's feet, Bonnie, the maker, wrote her name on her creation? It is as if to say, 'You are mine. I love you. I cherish you. I want to be with you.' Friends, do you realize that even *that* scene is an echo from a previous era?" My pastor opened his Bible and began quoting from the Old Testament prophet Isaiah: "But now thus says the LORD, he who created you, O Jacob, he who formed you, O Israel: 'Fear not, for I have redeemed you; I have called you by name, you are mine'" (Isaiah 43:1 ESV).

It suddenly occurred to me that I had never heard a more loving message from the pulpit. My pastor had preached not only about God's redemption of my actions but also about a total reclamation of my worthiness. This was the origin story of why we are so loved from the very beginning. I looked to my husband, who was equally entranced by the message. His initial awkward expression had softened to an empathic gaze at the photo of Bonnie's handwritten name on the screen.

The Carrot on a Stick

I realize that to this day the topic of worth still makes me anxious because of my personal trauma with domineering and abusive authority figures. In my experience, it is nearly impossible to hold on to one's self-worth when one is chronically at the mercy of an exploitative figure, whether that means a pastor-congregant relationship, a parent-child relationship, or any other relationship that has unequal power dynamics.

Think about the people in your life who have made you question your worth. It could be a controlling parent who often withheld love and demanded perfection or a verbally abusive boss who always makes excuses for their actions. It could also be a significant other who cheats on you and then tries to win you back with extravagant displays of affection. Some people may have experienced all three.

In the thick of my relationship with Josh, even when he was actively pursuing someone else, I made the conscious decision to stick by him no matter the cost. I know now that this is called being "trauma bonded." A trauma bond is a type of attachment that develops in response to repeated abuse or trauma, characterized by conflicting emotions of fear, love, and dependence.[1] It's a dangerous cycle of hope and despair, where the victim yearns for love and connection from the abuser, despite the harm they inflict.

This toxic bond can happen in any type of relationship where one person holds power over another, such as between partners, between hostages and kidnappers, or even between religious leaders and their followers. The promise of something better, always just out of reach, can trap many in the cycle of narcissistic abuse. Women and children are especially vulnerable to this dynamic. I, too, was caught in this cycle with Josh, leading to a loss of my self-worth.

I had a lightbulb moment when I stumbled upon a video by Dr. Ramani, a clinical psychologist and renowned authority on narcissism. It was then that I realized the link between my low self-worth and my attraction to narcissistic people. She explained:

> Over time, you're going to realize that you're actually "malnourished" when it comes to intimacy in a narcissistic relationship. The lack of deep connection, the lack of any interest in you, the superficiality, the avoidance of talking about any kinds of deep or emotional matters, can sneak up on you slowly. And when you attempt to address these issues, you will often face disrespect, resistance, denial, contempt, and gaslighting.[2]

Hearing this explanation provided a profound moment of clarity for me. The dots started connecting. Suddenly I saw the interconnections between my relationship with my mother, my relationship with Josh, and my lack of self-worth. I had gravitated toward Josh because he dangled the tantalizing prospect of emotional connection in front of me for months, showering me with sweet nothings, lavish displays of affection, and endless promises of a lifelong relationship. This was the only form of love I knew; it was all I had ever experienced.

Dr. Ramani's explanation jolted me with flashbacks of my high school years, when my mother physically abused and antagonized me, only to later try to apologize with wordless gestures of extravagant meals. Memories of her standing at the bathroom door, arms crossed, scrutinizing my body after every shower or change of clothes. Memories of her charming and sweet humor that seemed to make up for everything. Her love was the first carrot on a stick that I started chasing, and I hadn't stopped, even well into adulthood. Ultimately, my self-esteem became dependent on the approval of my narcissistic loved ones, and this dangerous mindset nearly pushed my sanity over the edge.

My feelings of incompetence, along with the shame and anger that followed, had a choke hold on my sense of worth. The chronic exposure to my mother's parenting style made me feel worthless, abandoned, and traumatized. Thankfully, through therapy sessions and studying the Scriptures for myself, I was slowly able to separate what was true from what was untrue. Therapy and the Word taught me the value of my intrinsic worth, even though this breakthrough didn't come easily.

I remember feeling bewildered and skeptical when my therapist validated the emotions I felt—even the ones I thought were shameful. I was skeptical of her character because the feeling of validation seemed so unfamiliar. I was used to people telling me I shouldn't feel a certain way, and I'd believe them. After every thought I put into words, I would follow up with, "Is that normal?" or "Is that okay?" My therapist would usually shrug her shoulders and say, "You tell *me* how you feel about it." After a month or so of my continual self-doubt, I remember her saying, "Hopefully, by the end of our time together, you will learn how to self-validate." Hearing that statement felt almost blasphemous because I was taught—both at home and at church—that I could not be trusted.

If you know what it's like to feel unworthy of being trusted, I invite you to seek counseling and explore the Scriptures on your own to see what God thinks about you. Without the meddling, critical voices that tell you how you should feel, I'm betting that God's voice will be much sweeter than you could imagine. For me, he stilled my doubts to a whisper and reassured me with his Word.

As you take the steps to explore your trauma with a licensed therapist and seek God earnestly through his Word, may you be empowered to break free from the cycle of seeking validation from others. I pray that this new perspective will fill you with hope for a future beyond your wildest expectations.

Running Away from Our Worthiness

After beautifully illustrating God's love for humanity through *Toy Story 4*, Pastor Tom queued up another clip from the movie. The sanctuary fell silent as the lights dimmed and the image of a sleeping Bonnie materialized on the big screen. With a sudden jolt of life, Forky sprang from Bonnie's grip and was immediately consumed by fear, anxiety, and insecurity. He frantically searched for the nearest garbage can to throw himself into. Despite being Bonnie's most treasured toy throughout the film, Forky struggled to accept his own worth and declared without hesitation, "I am not a toy! I was made for soup, salad, maybe chili, and then the trash!" What a startling reminder of our own habit of running away from our true worth.

Pastor Tom stopped the clip and reflected, "Sometimes the way we live or the thoughts we have in the quiet of the night communicates 'I am not God's treasure. I was made for school, work, maybe a nice little vacation, and then the grave.' But that's just not true. That's a lie straight from the pit of hell." The whole room fell quiet, and I looked to my right to see my husband frantically jotting down notes. I looked up as Pastor Tom went on:

> There's a false spirit embedded in that kind of mentality. It's actually the same false spirit you see in the Old Testament, demonstrated by King Saul. Do you know what the remedy was for King Saul when he was haunted by these lies? David, the anointed king-to-be, plays music and ministers to the current reigning king. Likewise, I want to say to everyone here today, if you feel haunted or tormented with lies that you are somehow not loved, that you are somehow *trash* and not treasure, then I want you to know that your Maker sings truth over you.

He quoted from the book of Zephaniah: "The LORD your God is in your midst, a mighty one who will save; he will rejoice over you with gladness; he will quiet you by his love; he will exult over you with loud singing" (Zephaniah 3:17 ESV). At this point, my eyes were already filled with tears. How was it that I had attended hundreds of church services in the twelve years I had been a Christian but hadn't ever heard this beautiful passage spoken over me from the pulpit? Why had I heard all the fire-and-brimstone passages highlighting my sin, shame, and imperfections multiple times over, but had never heard that God actually sings over me? I silently wept in my seat because it had taken this long for the message of worthiness to be spoken over me and these other beloved children of God. We are not trash; we are indeed God's treasures.

Accepting Our Worth

What if I told you right now that you have infinite worth in the eyes of God—that he loves you just as much as he loves Jesus? How does that make you feel?

- ☐ I feel ashamed and uncomfortable.
- ☐ I feel grateful and comforted.
- ☐ I feel indifferent.

For the first seven years in my walk with the Lord, I would have checked the first box without a doubt. I had so deeply internalized all the messages that told me I was bad and unworthy that I often felt like a burden to those around me. To stave off these feelings of worthlessness, I would try my best to earn people's love and acceptance by being as perfect as I possibly could. I was my own worst critic and was constantly filled with anxiety, like a personified Forky!

In a vulnerable self-help book titled *What Happened to You?*, Oprah Winfrey shared this discovery:

> What I've learned from talking to so many victims of trau-
> matic events, abuse, or neglect is that after absorbing these
> painful experiences, the child begins to ache. A deep longing
> to feel needed, validated, and valued begins to take hold. As
> these children grow, they lack the ability to set a standard for
> what they deserve. And if that lack is not addressed, what
> often follows is a complicated, frustrating pattern of self-
> sabotage, violence, promiscuity, or addiction.[3]

I, and so many of my childhood friends, lived out that pattern of self-sabotage, violence, promiscuity, and addiction to a
T—and it is the result of the way the enemy steals, kills, and
destroys the self-worth of the image bearers of God. We must
be resilient in our sense of worth by arming ourselves with the
truth of Jesus' teachings. If we pay attention to the things Jesus
says and the things God values throughout Scripture, it is clear
that he cherishes his creation. In the gospel of Luke, we read,
"Even the hairs on your head are all numbered. Do not be afraid;
you are more valuable than many sparrows" (Luke 12:7 NET).
Did you catch that? God paid so much attention to the details of
your making that he even knows the number of hairs on your
head. Your very existence brings him gladness because he made
you out of his great love.

The more I grow in my sense of worth, the more I realize
that God's message of worthiness is many times more powerful than the world's message of worthlessness. God's constant
loving adoration is what changes our hearts and encourages us
to repent, reclaim our worth, and radiate his love to others (see
Romans 2:4).

A Letter of Encouragement

The world often treats people as unworthy *before* they are born, while the church often treats people as unworthy *after* they are born. Sadly, these are two faces of the same coin. If people have infinite value in the eyes of God, then it doesn't matter what state they are in—born or unborn, nice or naughty, whole or broken. If we cannot earn our worth with good deeds, then we cannot lose our worth with bad deeds. Our worth has been given to us by God, who created us in his image.

If you have been one of the unlucky congregation members who was taught that you are inherently bad, I want you to understand that this teaching is taken completely out of context. There is a difference between inherent worth and the type of sinfulness that preachers often yell about. Our sinful nature has nothing to do with our worthiness in the eyes of God. Think of it this way: even if your child commits a hundred mistakes that break your heart, as their loving parent, you will still value them all the same. If you are a loving and healthy parent, there is nothing your child could do that would ever cause you to devalue them as your child.

God is the perfect and most loving parent. No matter how many heinous or self-destructive sins you've committed, your heavenly Father will always be willing to restore your honor and dignity the moment you run back into his arms. That extraordinary love is at the heart of the gospel and the reason that Jesus lovingly chose to carry our sins on the cross—to give us a restored relationship with him again. What a wild concept! The world wasn't prepared for such a love, and some still try to run away from it.

One of my vivid memories is of the day when I met a new friend named Becca,[*] who spoke to me about my worth. The

---

[*] "Becca" (pseud.).

If we cannot earn our worth with *good deeds,* then we cannot lose our worth with *bad deeds.*

conversation took place at a Chick-Fil-A, and her words left a lasting impact. After just ten or fifteen minutes of small talk and introductions, Becca took a deep breath and said, "All right, I feel like God has been telling me to share this with you the minute I prayed about you last night, but I was way too shy or embarrassed to say it. But he wants you to know you are already worthy." She flashed a hopeful smile at me, anticipating that it would ring a bell, but I didn't really know what to think of it. "That's really nice!" I mustered, still confused as to what she meant and why she said it. "Yeah," she said, "I hope that really sinks in with you! God loves you so, so much and he thinks you are already worthy." Again, I was unsure of how to respond. I didn't really know what being worthy meant. I supposed it was just some generic good feeling about yourself, which I thought I already had. "Hmm, thanks!" I said. Later, in the car with my other friend, I asked, "What was that all about?" and he chuckled as though to say, *Oh, you have no idea.*

Maybe you feel the same way after reading some of the

encouraging words in this chapter—words that sound nice and positive—but you have no idea what being infinitely worthy really means. That's all right, because worth is something you will ultimately learn by experience. After my strange encounter with Becca, I went back to normal life completely unchanged. I continued to strive to earn my worth in the eyes of others and lived a hypersensitive, hyperanxious life.

It wasn't until more than a year later that God reminded me of my encounter with Becca, and I broke down in tears. By then, I had already been in and out of the mental institution, finished my therapy sessions, switched churches, and moved out of my mother's house. It turned out that the Lord had a plan for me all along—a grand strategy to reinstate my worth as his beloved child. In his infinite wisdom, God knew what I needed before I even knew it myself, and he sent a sweet messenger like Becca to give me a heads-up for what was to come. I hope to be that kind of messenger for you. God says, "You are already worthy. I already love you so, so much. I have written my name on the soles of your feet. You are mine."

Open your heart to the idea that you are God's treasure. No matter how badly people have treated you or how badly you've treated yourself, God still sees you as valuable. You bear his very image! He has written his name on the soles of your feet, and you belong to him. You are his beloved. I speak from experience when I say that the more worthy you allow yourself to feel, the more resilient you will be in the face of adversity.

Reclaim your infinite worth by accepting God's love for you. His love is gentle and patient, not aggressive or overbearing. You can begin today by replacing the critical lies you believe about yourself with the truth of what God says about you. In the devotional journal I've written—*The Abundant Life Devotional Journal*—I created space for this exact exercise. Here's a sample of the exercise:

List three things society says about your worth in the left-hand column and respond with a biblical affirmation in the right-hand column. Here's a sample:

Society says: my worth is determined by my wealth.
God says: I am infinitely worthy.

Societal Expectations	Your God-Given Identity
1..............................	1..............................
2..............................	2..............................
3..............................	3..............................

Biblical Affirmations

- You are already loved beyond measure. (John 3:16)
- Nothing can make God love you less. (Romans 8:38–39)
- You are a child of God. (1 John 3:1)
- To God, you are worth Jesus' sacrifice. (Romans 5:8)
- You are fearfully and wonderfully made. (Psalm 139:14)
- God delights in you. (Psalm 18:19)
- You are inherently worthy despite your shortcomings. (Romans 5:8)
- You are made in the image of God. (Genesis 1:26)

There are dozens of other similar exercises in my first devotional book *The Abundant Life Devotional Journal*. Reflective activities such as journaling, going to therapy, or even talking with a trustworthy friend can help you reclaim your worth when facing adversity. By reading this chapter, you've already achieved the first step, which is to be aware of your infinite worth. Please take the words of this chapter as a message that the Lord wants you to hear. To him, you are infinitely worthy!

> **For you created my inmost being;**
> **you knit me together in my**
> **mother's womb.**
> **I praise you because I am fearfully**
> **and wonderfully made;**
> **your works are wonderful,**
> **I know that full well.**
>
> **PSALM 139:13–14 NIV**

Just for You

As you take in all that you've learned, remember to breathe and give yourself space to process. These reflection questions are designed to help you navigate your healing journey with greater clarity and insight. Whether you choose to explore them through journaling or in conversation with your small group, know that you are supported and accompanied by God's loving presence every step of the way.

1. How do you typically measure your self-worth?

2. What is the history behind this standard of measurement?
3. What one thing can you do this week to remind yourself of your infinite worth in Christ?

Let's Pray Together

Dear heavenly Father, I come to you today with a heart full of gratitude for your presence in my life. Please help me see myself the way you see me—as a precious and valuable child of God. I know that my worth is based not on my accomplishments, appearance, or the opinions of others, but on the fact that I am fearfully and wonderfully made in your image. Please guide me to fully embrace this truth and live a life that reflects your love and acceptance. Thank you for the infinite worth you have given me through Christ. In Jesus' name I pray. Amen.

Chapter 4

Belonging in
Your Tribe

Without going through that process of bonding,
we are doomed to alienation and isolation.
Not only do we not grow, we deteriorate.

Dr. Henry Cloud, *Changes That Heal*

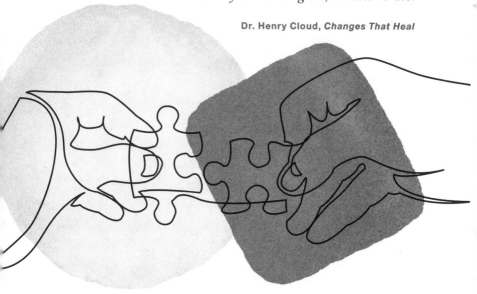

*I*n the past, establishing and maintaining healthy relationships has always been challenging. My trauma was rooted in toxic relationships, leading me to develop hypersensitivity and paranoia around being abandoned. However, this deep-seated fear was finally addressed in my first healthy adult relationship— the one with my therapist. Months later, I was blessed to meet a true friend who embodied the beautiful words of Proverbs: "There are 'friends' who destroy each other, but a real friend sticks closer than a brother" (Proverbs 18:24). Through this close friendship, I learned that trustworthy and safe people do exist and that I am capable of cultivating lasting bonds.

Little by little, I began to meet new people and open myself up to new church communities. I rejoiced whenever I found soulmates whom I wanted to keep forever—and ached when others left without so much as an explanation. But the more practice I got at maintaining deep bonds, the better I became. Eventually, I found myself surrounded by the most supportive tribe of people I ever could have prayed for.

It all began when my husband and I were invited to a private tea-tasting event in early 2021 hosted by my friend Joanne.* Normally, I would shy away from events like these (no matter how small the group) because of my general social anxiety. This time, I pushed myself to go because it felt like the right thing to do. So off we went, to a charmingly curated boutique on the outskirts of the Silver Lake neighborhood in Los Angeles, where

---

* "Joanne" (pseud.).

we were joined by two other couples and a single woman. We were an eclectic mix of individuals from across the globe, but our paths converged at Joanne's table. We opened up to each other about our deepest desires and aspirations, family challenges, and career pitfalls. And then something remarkable happened: we paused to pray together, lifting each other up and supporting one another with unwavering love and kindness. It was a microcosm of what church is supposed to be like.

Halfway through the serendipitous meeting, an Argentinian woman named Alma** looked me dead in the eye and said, "Hey, I feel like I know you." I thought she meant I felt familiar to her, to which I replied, "I feel like I've known you for a long time too!" "No," she said, "I think I know your face. Do you make videos on YouTube?" I was taken aback because Alma had only moved to LA a few months earlier. It turned out she had watched one of my devotional videos while still living in Argentina, and that single video inspired her to move to Los Angeles in pursuit of God's calling. She had left everything behind—her family, businesses, and home—out of a desire to minister to people in the city of LA. And now God had brought us together to this mini "church service" of a tea-tasting event in the heart of LA so we could meet face-to-face. I was left speechless by God's beautiful orchestration.

A few weeks later, Alma invited me and my husband, Jon, to her house for a dinner party. As we arrived at the stunning house, we were welcomed by a warm glow of twinkling fairy lights on the front patio. Upon entering, we were absolutely amazed by the incredible showcase of art and vintage decor that surrounded us. It felt as if we had stepped into another world—like Narnia. As I wandered through the enchanting Edwardian-style living room, I felt an inexplicable sensation. It was as if the presence of God had

---

** "Alma" (pseud.).

gently brushed against me. We made our way to the magnificent dining area, and I knew this was going to be a truly unforgettable experience. The dining setup was no less vivid than the painting *The Last Supper* itself. "This place is crazy," Jon whispered to me. "I know," I said. "I can't believe we're still in LA."

The House of Miracles

At the time, Jon and I were planning to host our own small group at our apartment in the suburbs. While we hadn't worked out the logistics yet, we felt strongly that God wanted us to invest our time in discipling people. When Alma brought out an incredible array of home-cooked Argentinian food and served us so generously that evening, I had an idea. "Would you be willing to host our small group at your house?" I asked. Without missing a beat, she responded, "Of course! With pleasure. Invite anyone you want. We are all family here."

It was a done deal, orchestrated by none other than the Lord himself. One moment, the sweet woman was watching my vlogs in Argentina, and the next moment, we were in the same small group, praying for each other and breaking bread together. I approached the buffet table to gather some side dishes while still in awe of how incredible our meeting had been. As I glanced up, my eyes fell on a sign that read "The House of Miracles." What a confirmation!

The next day, I listed our small group opportunity on the church website. I uttered a short prayer, hit Enter, and hoped for the best. I didn't think many people would show up because our church had dozens of available small groups at the time. During the first official meetup, a steady stream of new faces arrived at the enormous doors: a couple from Mauritius, a man from Kenya, a couple from Texas, a woman from Iowa, and so many others from our church. The House of Miracles was packed.

Everyone who walked through those doors was treated like family. There was always a seat at the table for them, no matter how cramped. Gathering in that eclectic house in the heart of Los Angeles, we feasted on home-cooked meals, lifted our voices in worship, and stood in the gap for each other whenever needed. It was an unlikely group of individuals brought together by the power of the divine, and now they have become my tribe. Their stories and experiences have opened my eyes to the boundless love and compassion described in the book of Acts. When our brother from Mauritius was involved in a terrible motorcycle accident, our community immediately put its plans on hold and rushed him to the hospital without a second thought. By the end of that year, even the most guarded person at the table had opened up and shared their deepest vulnerabilities with the group. We had become a chosen family.

Sometimes all it takes to find your tribe is to say yes. If I hadn't said yes to the spontaneous tea-tasting event, I wouldn't have met Alma or had the small group of committed friends I have now. It may have taken me thirty years to learn how to properly steward relationships like these, but God's timing could not have been better. If the opportunity had come five years earlier, I doubt I would've had the boldness to accept. But with his unwavering patience, God transformed my once-hardened heart into one of flesh. He gave me the ability to trust in new relationships and fortified my resilience in the face of the unknown. God orchestrated everything in advance and gently invited me to participate in his gathering of saints. Through my wonderfully diverse small group, I learned the true meaning of unconditional belonging. And for the first time in a long time, I remembered what it felt like to be forever home.

In *What Happened to You?*, Dr. Bruce Perry explains, "Without connection to people who care for you, spend time with you, and support you, it is almost impossible to step away from any form

You need to *find* those who can fully *accept* you for who you are and *embrace* you on your journey to *wholeness*.

of unhealthy reward and regulation . . . Connectedness counters the pull of addictive behaviors. It is the key."[1] Human connection truly is the key to counteracting the effects of traumatic experiences. When you're struggling with depression, anxiety, or addiction stemming from trauma, isolating yourself until you feel ready to reemerge isn't the answer. Instead, it's crucial to heal within the safe confines of a supportive community.

Being plugged into a group that genuinely cares for you can help you learn healthy coping mechanisms. Over time, the reward system in your brain shifts from craving unhealthy habits to craving the nourishing reward of human connection. You need to find your tribe—those who can fully accept you for who you are and embrace you on your journey to wholeness. This type of support can come in a variety of group settings as well as in one-on-one relationships that allow you to see the breadth of what relationships can be. The foundation of true healing and restoration is a personal relationship with Christ, who then works through our communities to show us his love in real, tangible ways.

Beauty for Ashes

I know what it's like to want to avoid close relationships altogether out of fear that the past will repeat itself. Growing up in a household with a history of domestic violence and emotional abuse left me hesitant to form deep connections with new people. When I did reach out, I found myself feeling anxious, irritable, and insecure. If this sounds familiar, please know you are not cursed; you are simply dealing with the aftermath of trauma.

It's easy to question how a relationship as tumultuous as the one I had with my mother could possibly be redeemed. The wounds run deep, and the trauma is palpable. When our mothers fail us in fundamental ways, it can damage the very core of our ability to form secure attachments with ourselves, God, and others. However, there is hope. Just as a relationship can cause great harm to a person, it can also be a source of healing and restoration.

In 2019, I took the plunge and moved into a high-rise apartment in the heart of downtown LA all by myself. This was the perfect opportunity for me to start my own YouTube channel and share the wisdom and insights I had been gaining from my renewed relationship with God. As I poured out my heart and soul into my devotional videos, I found myself experiencing a sense of peace and security I had never felt before. It was a deep and abiding sense of calm, a feeling of abundance that can only come from being fully at peace with the Lord.

I couldn't help but yearn for my mother to experience this same peace and freedom. Despite the terrible things she and I had gone through, the physical distance between us made it easier for me to process my pain, and my therapy sessions had helped me to accept her for who she is. I also found solace in my close-knit community at church, which provided the emotional and spiritual support I needed to make tough decisions, such as discerning whether I should reconcile with my mother. After much prayer and wise counsel, I decided to set a goal to give my mother the gift of early retirement.

Although our relationship was complicated during my high school years and beyond, I was able to understand my mother's situation as a single, widowed parent in a foreign country where she did not speak the language. She must have felt panicked, abandoned, and lonely during the earlier years of my father's passing. Though there will never be justification for harming me, I understood that her abusive behaviors came from a place of ignorance and perpetuated trauma rather than a place of callous hatred. She loved me deeply; she just struggled to love me well. When I discovered that healing was possible with the right measures in place, such as having a stable foundation of love and a supportive community that respects my boundaries, I was convicted to share this gift with my mother, who needed it desperately.

I also feel a need to mention that reconciliation is not always possible or advisable, depending on your situation. If you're dealing with an abusive or unsafe person who continues to threaten your peace and safety, the wisest path to take may be to love them from afar by praying for them while maintaining your healthy boundaries. Reconciliation requires both sides to show up with love and a willingness to change for the sake of the relationship. Otherwise, you're gluing a shattered vase back together without all the pieces. It may look all right at first glance, but it won't be functional.

With this in mind, I decided to initiate a process of reconciliation with my mother to see if it was even possible. I had long prayed for her to be released from survival mode and to start living a life of true peace and fulfillment. My goal, then, was to show her that she is loved and accepted, and to point her toward the path of healing. The first step was to help her break free from survival mode.

I made this goal known to my best friend, who offered to manage the business side of things while I continued to create my devotional videos on YouTube. And just like that, we were on a mission to nudge my mother into retirement.

After months of working hard and saving up, I met my financial goals. I planned a great surprise for my mother and invited her to my apartment under the guise of filming a spring roll video. While she happily ate her spring rolls, I pivoted the camera toward her and handed her a handwritten note—written in my broken Vietnamese. She looked visibly confused but went along with it anyway.

Hi, Mom,

I know we didn't get along well during my teenage years, but now that I'm older, I can see how hard it must have been for you. You had to take care of me all by yourself in a country where you don't speak the language. I won't lie, you were pretty intense when I was in high school, but I know you went through a lot. You were raised by a crazy man, your own family members betrayed you, your husband passed away too early, and your body was broken from multiple surgeries.

But I want you to know that you still have Jesus, and that is enough. Jesus had mercy on you. He changed my heart and convicted me to take care of you. From now on, you don't have to work anymore. You've retired early! I will pay for all your bills and expenses. You can go on vacation now. It's not a burden for me, so please accept it. I love you, Mom!

Your daughter,

Anh

She read my note aloud with tears in her eyes and then completely broke down at the end. I ran over to her side and hugged her, grateful that we were able to share the beginnings of reconciliation in our lifetime. Generations of hurt, loss, and love converged and found their ultimate redemption in that very moment. It was a powerful experience that gave us the sense of closure we both longed for.

After I extended this olive branch, our relationship shifted into something entirely different. Our dynamic felt foreign but much gentler and sweeter than before. We were finally learning how to have a functional mother-daughter relationship for the first time since I became a young adult. This reconciliation only could have happened after I gained other healthy relationships and built a solid understanding of my worth. The foundation of love and worthiness that God had laid in my life freed me to show grace to my mother. I no longer needed her to affirm my value; instead, I wanted to show her how valuable *she* was in the eyes of God.

The prophet Isaiah wrote of the idea of exchanging beauty for ashes:

He has sent me to tell those who mourn
that the time of the Lord's favor has come,

and with it, the day of God's anger against
  their enemies.
To all who mourn in Israel,
  he will give a crown of beauty for ashes,
a joyous blessing instead of mourning,
  festive praise instead of despair.
In their righteousness, they will be like great oaks
  that the LORD has planted for his own glory.

Isaiah 61:2–3

This prophecy shows the sweetness of God's character. His heart is soft toward his mourning children. Rather than scoffing at our pain or being emotionally detached, God leans in closer. He bends down to listen to our cries. To soothe his children, he gives them a crown of beauty in exchange for their anguish, a promise of joy after their grief, and an uplifting celebration instead of despair. God promises hope to those who mourn so that they might become stronger after their pain.

Even though it hurt God to see my mother treat me the way she did, he saw something deeper in her heart that no one else could see: he saw her grief and had compassion on her. In his great mercy, he opened my eyes to the true pain underneath and allowed both of us to experience the peace we had desperately longed for.

Without the support of my therapist and godly friends, I wouldn't have had the emotional capacity to extend this olive branch to my mother. Knowing that I had other people to love, guide, and support me gave me the courage to take the risk of reconciling. Because of the emotional resilience I had built from being in a supportive community, the cycle of grief between my mother and me finally came to a gentle halt. From that moment of reconciliation onward, there was finally space for beauty, joy, and festive celebration between us. Like the great oaks that God planted with his own hands for his own glory, we were able to move forward from our grief and into posttraumatic growth.

Posttraumatic Growth

Posttraumatic growth (PTG), sometimes called posttraumatic wisdom, is the mental resilience and wisdom that result from making peace with one's traumatic experiences. Posttraumatic growth can occur without professional intervention like psychotherapy, but therapy can certainly help speed up the process. A person can experience PTG in five ways:[2]

1. **Education:** Being informed about our trauma through personal research, formal education, or other means of learning.
2. **Emotional regulation:** Learning to contain our overwhelming emotions until we are ready to respond.
3. **Disclosure:** Being able to speak about our trauma to an empathetic person or group.
4. **Narrative development:** Making sense of our pain in the grand scheme of our story.
5. **Service:** Using what we've learned from our experiences to benefit the lives of others.

I've had the privilege of experiencing all five facilitations through the healthy relationships I've cultivated. With my therapist, I was *educated* on the effects of my trauma and developed the tools to help me *regulate* my emotions. Through my small group, I was able to *speak* about my trauma in a safe and accepting environment. Through my relationship with God, I was able to derive *purpose* from my pain and ultimately make use of my experiences by *helping others* through my writing and social media ministry.

The growth and wisdom that came from my pain all happened within the context of relationships. I believe the same is true for most people who have moved forward from their trauma to experience the benefits of PTG. We simply do not heal in isolation. For any kind of healing to occur, we must have a connection with at least one human being who is willing to listen to us and care for us.

A Divine Restoration

At the dawn of creation, it wasn't atoms or galaxies that mattered most; it was God's bond with human beings that held the greatest significance to him. He had you in mind when the earth was still formless and his Spirit was hovering over the waters (see Genesis 1:2, 26). He had you in mind before he created the light and the darkness, the flora and the fauna. He had you in mind before the creation of the world, the fall that ensued, the mercy he would show, and the cross he would bear. God has always wanted a relationship with you. He built the physical world just to have a home with you.

May you find comfort and healing in knowing that your heart can be softened toward your gentle Creator, no matter how scarred you may be from past relationships. Let Jesus, who is always present, bring you peace and joy and quiet your heart with his love. Know that he delights in you and rejoices over you with loud singing. God desires a relationship with you, and he will do whatever it takes to restore you to wholeness. With him as your guide and anchor, you can feel at home wherever you are. And when he brings people into your life who show you his love and kindness, may you find the courage to welcome them in and experience the beauty of a healthy community.

> The LORD your God is in your midst,
> a mighty one who will save;
> he will rejoice over you with
> gladness;
> he will quiet you by his love;
> he will exult over you with loud
> singing.

ZEPHANIAH 3:17 ESV

Just for You

Take a moment to pause and reflect on all you've learned. Don't rush through this moment of reflection. Take a deep breath and allow yourself the time and space to process. When you're ready, take some time to reflect on the prompts below.

1. Can you describe a time when someone affirmed your worth? How did it make you feel? Use the 100 Emotions Word Bank in the back of this book to help you identify your feelings.
2. Name one person who makes you feel safe and understood. If you don't have access to a healthy community, feel free to reach out to the contacts listed in the back of this book.
3. Which of the five approaches to gaining posttraumatic growth resonates with you most, and why?

Dear heavenly Father, thank you for walking alongside me as I find my tribe. Please help me connect with people who will love me and show up for me. Help me to be brave and open-minded in my search and to trust that you will guide me to the people who will be my allies in this journey of healing. May all of my relationships shape me to look more like your Son, Jesus. In his name I pray. Amen.

Chapter 5

Becoming Who You Were Meant to Be

Purpose is a powerful thing. It will have you walking around in life like you belong there.

Nakeia Homer

*M*ost of us have intrinsic knowledge that we were created for *something*, but our sense of purpose often feels distant or buried. Struggles such as traumatic stress, sickness, relationship complexities, or even physical trauma can greatly cloud our sense of purpose. Have you ever noticed that when someone is depressed, it seems as though they've temporarily lost their sense of direction? Even if the person is a Christian and cognitively knows what their purpose should be, life challenges and emotional overwhelm can dull the passion and sense of purpose of even the most faithful Christians.

No amount of reasoning seems to work when someone is living with the effects of trauma, and it turns out there's an actual, physical reason for this. Current research shows that the prefrontal cortex of our brain temporarily shuts down when we encounter traumatic stress.[1] I remember times when I was triggered by relational conflict and couldn't think of anything other than simply hiding from what I perceived as danger. Life purpose was the last thing I could process when I was in survival mode. I didn't have the energy or clarity to think about anything beyond my immediate needs.

The prefrontal cortex is responsible for conscious self-control, reasoning, making sense of language, and knowing the difference between the past, present, and future, among other things. This means that when it temporarily shuts down, as in the case of posttraumatic stress disorder (PTSD) strugglers and anyone else who experiences traumatic stress, you lose the ability to think rationally, speak clearly, behave logically, or even perceive time.[2] Your body goes into a state of defense, shutting down or roiling up as though you are reliving the same danger that traumatized you to begin with. In this state of survival, your brain makes the executive decision to block out any unnecessary functions, which includes the ability to perceive abstract ideas such as purpose and your sense of self.

This essentially means you shouldn't blame yourself for feeling lost after a lifetime or a season of crises. Whether you've been deeply wounded by a stranger or by a family member, your survival mode will kick in and your brain will temporarily shut down your ability to think abstractly. You are neither a bad person nor a spiritually inept person for not having a sense of purpose. You may simply be in survival mode. Your brain has been doing exactly what God has designed it to do—keep you alive.

Breaking Free from Survival Mode

When people are in survival mode and their frontal lobe shuts down, they are pumped full of stress hormones that add to their agitation and irritability. This can explain why first-generation immigrant parents like mine hardly ever thought about such concepts as purpose and identity on a day-to-day basis. Most of their focus was spent on keeping their family alive in a foreign land. Even a dreamer like my father had to put his dreams aside and embrace being in "survival mode" when we moved to America.

The problem was, of course, that my parents' survival mentality showed up in abusive patterns of behavior, such as being overly controlling, condescending, and physically violent. An already abusive household can get even worse when the main providers are in survival mode.

As in the case of my immigrant family, any minor infraction or unforeseen event was treated as the highest level of threat. Our Sundays were invariably a dedicated day for stressful arguments and violent outbursts between my parents. Like clockwork, my adolescent self would cower and hide in the corner of our bedroom as soon as I sensed any minor shift in my parents' dynamics. They fought often about money and religion, but any trivial topic could set them off. In order to survive, I learned how to anticipate danger before it even appeared. My keen pulse on the mood of our home served me well later in life after my father died and my mother shifted her temper manifestations toward me.

However, as soon as my serious relationship with Josh ended, my strong survival instincts became more damaging than helpful. He cemented my fear of abandonment and heightened my distrust of people. My mind was on high alert for imminent danger, even when nothing bad was happening around me. Like my parents, I was easily set off by any minor infraction or threat to my sense of control. When I was triggered by the people I subsequently dated, I would nearly black out from my fits of rage, thrashing about violently like an overgrown toddler.

It was a deeply shameful and terrifying experience to feel like I had no control over my reactions. I had frequent disturbing dreams and flashbacks that made me scared and angry. The closer I got to someone, the more unsafe I felt. I slowly became a replica of the terrifying and abusive mother I feared in high school.

This is what survival mode can do to you when you employ it out of context. Not being able to enjoy your current blessings because you're anticipating the next disaster is a clear sign of trauma. The hypervigilance that had kept me safe as a child was now keeping me stuck in a cycle of distrust and fear in my relationships.

When I was in college, I finally brought my concerns to a therapist. The therapist took out a checklist of sorts and read a list of questions, which caught me off guard because I felt like she was reading my mind. In the end, she said, "You got nearly the highest score for all of the symptoms of someone with PTSD." My stomach sank because I thought PTSD was reserved for military veterans and people who have gone through "extreme trauma" (whatever that meant to me). Living in survival mode was a sign that I was battling something far more profound than a few panic attacks I had convinced myself were the root of the problem. I was carrying the weight of my past without realizing it, as I thought that the chaos and pain of my childhood were just part of life. But as I began to unpack the layers of my trauma, I discovered I had been conditioned to accept a version of reality that was far from normal.

If you're feeling empty and purposeless today, I want to encourage you to have compassion for yourself. To make sense of an abstract concept like purpose, the prefrontal cortex must be focused and engaged. You must be in a calm state of mind and feel safe to think and behave rationally. Acknowledge that part of you for doing its best, and let it know that it no longer needs to intrude into the situations you find yourself in. You are entering a safer space, where you can breathe more slowly, let your shoulders relax, and unclench your jaw. You don't have to be on high alert. You can thrive. Let me show you how.

To get out of survival mode and allow your brain to deepen its belief in your inherent worth and the possibility of finding purpose, you will need help. The following tools should help activate your prefrontal cortex and possibly alleviate PTSD symptoms. It's essential to get this help so you can reengage your sense of purpose and build a more stable foundation for your new life. Here are some tools I've found helpful:

1. **Therapy.** There are many different forms of psychotherapy that work for people, such as talk therapy (also called cognitive behavioral therapy), IFS (internal

family systems), and EMDR (eye movement desensitiza-tion reprocessing). In many parts of the United States, you can have access to therapists from almost any cultural background and religion. Seeking therapy for the first time can seem like a daunting task, but I assure you it will pay off in the long run. Getting help from a good therapist provides a safe space to process life's challenges, learn more about yourself through the context of your childhood, and adopt tools to help you cope with your stressors.

2. **Mentorship and community.** Healing is not a solitary journey; it requires the warmth of community and the compassion of others. The power of collective support and love can be transformative, reminding us that we are not alone in our struggles. Having a community of peers who accept, uplift, and celebrate you can help you build mental resilience and cope with life's unpredictability.

3. **Journaling.** Journaling has numerous documented benefits for your healing journey, some of which include helping you reflect on past events, process hurtful experiences, and set hopeful goals for the future. This is precisely why I created *The Abundant Life Devotional Journal*—to help people put words to their emotions and process their daily experiences through prayerful guides and reflections. My hope is that people will rediscover their sense of identity and purpose when they calmly gather their complex thoughts in one place.

4. **Exercise and sleep.** Much of the physical distress we feel on a daily basis can be eased with a healthy amount of exercise and sleep. When we stay moderately active for at least thirty minutes a day, our brains secrete chemicals called endorphins that can reduce stress, improve our

mood, and give us a better night's rest.[3] Never under-estimate the effects of quality sleep and a healthy exercise routine on your overall mood and well-being. The more resilient your physical body feels, the more mental resil-ience you will have as a result. The next time you find yourself feeling overwhelmed or triggered, try going for a walk in nature or practicing breathing exercises. Notice how the ground feels beneath your feet, the texture of the foliage around you, and the patterns in the sky. Notice how the rhythm of walking affects your heart rate, the palms of your hands, and your shoulders—or any of the areas that are typically most affected by your emotions. By being mindful of your senses, you remind your body that it is grounded in the present and not stuck back where the danger used to be.

5. **Rhythmic hobbies.** After I moved out of my mother's house, I suddenly felt the urge to take on a host of different hobbies. It wasn't to distract myself from my unpleasant memories but rather to help me stay inspired and regulated while learning new skills I enjoy. By picking up rhythmic hobbies such as painting, singing, dancing, and garden-ing, I taught myself how to self-soothe in productive—as opposed to destructive—ways. My YouTube channel is filled with soothing and cathartic videos on creative hobbies that provide ways for people to feel peaceful and relaxed in their own company. Sometimes all it takes to make life seem less scary is to put our hands in the dirt and feel the earth that our heavenly Father created.

These are five of the most effective changes I made to reen-gage my prefrontal cortex and feel safe enough to approach God and others again.

Safety in Proximity

You may be surprised that the vast majority of this chapter doesn't focus on your actual purpose at all. That's because you cannot fully live out your God-given purpose without a foundation of safety and security. So my goal here is to highlight ways to create the right conditions for recognizing and following your purpose, so that your pursuit of your purpose becomes more than just an intellectual one. Only when your heart feels safe and secure can you truly embrace your purpose and live it out fully.

Take a few minutes to rest in the knowledge of God's unconditional love for you. How does it feel to know that he loves you without reservations and that his love is trustworthy and safe? Imagine yourself basking in the shadow of his wings. Feel the grandeur of his presence—how much bigger he is than your biggest obstacles. He promises to protect you as you walk alongside him. Does this experience feel safe to you, or are you distrustful of it?

It's okay if you don't feel completely safe in the presence of God. That's why the five tools above are so important; they can help ground your anxieties and bring back your sense of safety.

I remember hitting rock bottom with my anxiety and depression after finishing university and moving back into my mother's house, even though I had been a Christian for several years. The pain I experienced during this period of my life was like a recurring nightmare of the anxiety and depression I faced in high school, but even more pronounced. This time, I felt abandoned by God. Because I was back in survival mode, I lost all sense of the purpose and passion I had gained when I encountered Christ.

In the stillness of my therapist's dim office, I was asked to close my eyes and imagine Jesus there in the same room as the two of us. I said, "Okay," and then I sensed my whole body seize up.

My therapist said, "Now open your eyes. Where do you picture Jesus to be?"

I shrugged my shoulders. "I don't really know. Not anywhere in particular. Maybe in that corner over there." I pointed to the plant near the door.

She nodded empathetically, and we proceeded to talk about my life's timeline, dissecting each memory that caused a visceral reaction in me. She didn't bring up the Jesus thing again until much later.

At the time, I was working at a local nonprofit for a domineering boss named Wendell.* He was a larger-than-life commander of his church and nonprofit for more than thirty years. Wendell threw extraordinary feasts for his congregation, held exuberant galas for his nonprofit, and spoke with such authority that I once heard his own daughter say, "I just assume that whatever he says is the word of God." At the time, I couldn't agree more.

Occasionally, I'd catch glimpses of him calling people morons and saying some harsh things about certain congregation members, but I chalked it up to his quirkiness and continued to take his side because he had treated me like a daughter for the years I had known him. Wendell proclaimed to be my spiritual father, after all. I didn't expect him to be perfect; I just expected him to be loving. And for years, he was.

When I applied to work at the nonprofit after graduation, I realized that my relationship with Wendell had taken a nosedive.

With the added stress of diminished tithes and donations, Wendell was considerably more irritable than before. The catastrophizing and gossiping I once attributed to quirkiness now became an unbearable daily occurrence. He began slamming tables during work meetings, calling us idiots and morons, and making sly, condescending comments to indicate his stress and

---

* "Wendell" (pseud.).

disapproval. Still, I encouraged myself to keep the same optimistic and free-spirited charisma I'd always shown toward him. I believed he was still my spiritual father, despite being my stressed-out boss, and I thought that fathers were supposed to be gentle, lavish in their love, and forgiving.

With this same free-spirited approach, I behaved in a way that reflected my feelings of safety. I took calculated risks, was solution-oriented, and flexed my creativity in my work projects. I helped the nonprofit gain more donors in one campaign than they had gained the entire previous three years. I thought my performance would win back the old Wendell I knew—the one who fed us lavishly, cracked hilarious dad jokes, and embraced us through our shortcomings. It didn't happen.

One day, I was summoned to his office to update him on a marketing campaign. The tension in the workplace was at an all-time high due to his unpredictable nature, and it was only a matter of time before I knew we had to talk about it. After an oddly quick catch-up, Wendell said, "You know, I'm your boss, but I'm also your pastor. You can come to me when you're not happy about something I said at work. You can even confide in me and say, 'I hate my boss!' because after work, I'm your senior pastor." I nodded and then got out of that office as quickly as I could.

I ran to the back of the building, sat on the steps, and sobbed. I couldn't tell what was real or imaginary anymore. I suddenly felt trapped, as though my entire world were being micromanaged, critiqued, and mocked. The same man who proclaimed himself to be my spiritual father was verbally abusing me every week, and I was expected to confide in that man about his "other self." I thought back on God's many names, such as the Great Physician, Wonderful Counselor, and Prince of Peace, and a rush of anger welled up inside my chest. I decided at that moment that I no longer wanted anything to do with egotistical men who assigned themselves unsolicited roles in my life.

Later that week, I updated my therapist about the details of our exchange, and she shook her head in disbelief. Indulging in her empathy felt like a radical act of resistance. I had become so accustomed to having my feelings invalidated that experiencing empathy felt like a rare and precious gift.

It took another month of therapy for me to stop questioning my own worth, and another six months to consider finding a new job, moving out of my mother's house, and leaving my beloved church. Once I finally acted and distanced myself from these stressors, my sense of purpose slowly came back. My therapist must have noticed a consistent difference in my mood because during one of our final meetings, she asked me to close my eyes and envision Jesus in the room again. I did as she said and felt my palms resting comfortably by my side.

"Where is he standing in the room?" she asked.

After pausing for a moment, I answered, "He's actually sitting next to me."

Despite the many years of torment of living under my mother's roof and the alarming experiences at the nonprofit, my therapist was the first person to successfully challenge me to fearlessly trust people again. Thanks to her gentle nudging and wisdom, I slowly made my way back to the heavenly Father—my actual spiritual Father. What I found at the end of my journey wasn't a disappointed parent, like my mother, or a disapproving authority, like Wendell, but a deeply compassionate Father who ran toward me with arms wide open. *He's safe*, I thought. *I'm finally home.*

Friends, I want you to know you are safe in the loving presence of your Creator, who wants nothing more than to have a restored relationship with you. He is not forceful or disrespectful; he will not barge his way into your space without your invitation. As you continue to process the traumas in your life, Jesus will remain near for the day when you are finally ready to invite him in again. His patience is boundless because he loves you deeply. Take your time to unpack the hurt, little by little, and watch as your relationship with Jesus naturally becomes more authentic and intimate than ever before. This restored relationship with your Creator will make it possible for you to process your God-given purpose.

How to Be Purpose-Full

According to the Merriam-Webster dictionary, purpose is defined as "something set up as an object or end to be attained: intention." In the Christian perspective, it is not a matter of *creating* your own purpose (as we experience in Western culture), nor is it *living up* to your familial or social duties (as we see in Eastern culture). Rather, it's about accepting God's purpose for you. God's purpose should come *before* self-actualization and societal expectations.

The first time I was introduced to the topic of purpose was in my high school English class. After assigning the class Albert Camus's existentialist novel *The Stranger*, my English teacher engaged us in the topic of self-created purpose. Even as an agnostic fifteen-year-old, I felt that the concept of self-created purpose made no real sense. It certainly came off as being empowering, but the idea seemed illogical to me. Nothing that has been created has ever given itself purpose. The purpose of creation lies in the *intention* of the Creator, as we will soon explore.

Accepting God's love is just the beginning of building a solid foundation for your life. The next step is to embrace your God-given purpose. When a new home is built, the structure of the foundation must be carefully calculated for the total weight of the house. Otherwise, the structure will weaken over time and the home could sink or collapse. Right now, you are in the process of fortifying your foundation. Understanding and believing in your purpose will not only help you feel focused and fulfilled but also keep you standing firm when trials come your way.

In any real-life circumstance, it is always the creator who gives the invention its purpose. This is no different from us and our Creator. When we set off on a path to find purpose outside of our Creator, we end up filling the void with things that can never truly satisfy. Even if those things can be good, such as family, money, and status, these peripheral blessings cannot quench our thirst for purpose. We will always end up wanting more.

Our true purpose has three layers: spiritual, physical, and vocational. Understanding each layer will help us build a foundation on Christ's love rather than on our painful history.

Your Trifold Purpose

1. Your Spiritual Purpose

Think of the innermost layer, your spiritual purpose, as the foundational layer behind everything you do. Before you can start doing anything, you must learn simply how to *be*. Your purpose in life starts with accepting that you are loved by God. Period.

To some, simply being loved hardly sounds like a purpose at

all because it doesn't involve doing anything. Yet remember that the object of creation doesn't give itself purpose; it derives purpose from the intentions of its Creator. In the book of Revelation, we get a glimpse into the gathering of the twenty-four elders, who placed their crowns before the enthroned God and cried out, "You are worthy, O Lord our God, to receive glory and honor and power. For you created all things, and they exist because you created what you pleased" (Revelation 4:11). The Scriptures tell us that God created what he pleased, and that includes you and me!

Accepting God's unconditional love is the first step toward fulfilling your spiritual purpose and grants you a remarkable resilience.

More specifically, the book of Romans reminds us, "Everything comes from him and exists by his power and is intended for his glory. All glory to him forever! Amen" (Romans 11:36). In other words, our very existence brings glory to God! To simply exist as the object of God's love is in itself purposeful, and accepting his unconditional love is the first step toward fulfilling your spiritual purpose. It also grants you a remarkable resilience in the face of life's trials. As we saw in chapter 2 ("You Are Loved"), grounding yourself in the understanding that you are divinely cherished lays a sturdy foundation for a life of purpose and fulfillment.

2. Your Physical Purpose

The Bible declares that in the beginning, human beings were commissioned to "fill the earth and subdue it" (Genesis 1:28 NIV). There are two parts to our physical purpose: filling the earth with other followers of Christ and doing our part to sustain the planet.

Some interpretations emphasize the "fill the earth" task as referring only to the bearing of children, but that isn't the only way to fulfill your physical purpose. Keep in mind that people were already having trouble conceiving as early as the days of Abraham. The heart of this command is reflected in the life of

Jesus; he had no children of his own but showed the love of God to everyone he met. If bearing children is not possible for you, you can still fulfill the first half of your physical purpose by filling the world with more worshipers of Christ. In other words, the people you disciple can become your spiritual sons and daughters.

The second half of your physical purpose is to have dominion over the earth. Unfortunately, because we live in a fallen world, human beings no longer subdue the earth as much as they destroy it. Despite the disturbing decline of our planet, we have a responsibility to develop a world that honors God and brings him glory. Stewardship starts with you. From the small things such as recycling to larger things such as using green technology to help our planet, we should always aim to steward the earth well and fulfill our physical purpose in that regard. By taking care of our planet, we will gain a greater sense of connectedness with our physical home. This act of stewardship will also boost our resilience and heighten our sense of ownership over our lives—something we often lose when we feel helpless in our trauma. Our physical purpose is perhaps the most grounding layer of all three.

3. Your Vocational Purpose

Your vocational purpose is the least vital of the three layers, and yet it's the layer that people tend to fixate on the most when their sense of purpose is discussed. Your vocation is not limited to traditional career paths but also includes any main job or responsibility the Lord has entrusted you with (full-time parenting or overseas missions, for example).

Understanding *why* you are called to a particular job can be just as important as pursuing the job itself. God calls many people to a multitude of different jobs—sometimes a different one for each season. If we treat our job as nothing more than a means of self-fulfillment and self-actualization, it is not a calling; it is simply something that serves our own self-interest.

However, if we acknowledge that God placed us where we are in this season for his glory and purpose, and we work diligently as though we're working for God and not for other human beings (Colossians 3:23), then our pursuit of God's calling can have an eternal impact on both ourselves and others.

Bringing Purpose to Your Pain

I once uploaded a "failed" makeover to YouTube, hoping that the lessons I learned would resonate with someone out there. It was the first makeover I had done in a while, so I miscalculated a few materials and didn't double-check the packages I received, which resulted in the delivery of a few wrong products. The whole thing turned out to be a mess, no matter how much I tried to white-knuckle my way through.

After running into multiple roadblocks, I finally took a minute to rest and consult with the Lord. Despite my prayers for things to go smoother, they didn't, and in the end, I learned a valuable lesson on how to let go. When I decided to take a step back from my troubles rather than fight against them, I was able to observe how God was exposing my sense of perfectionism and pride. I kept the makeover video as it was—unfinished and filled with flaws—and shared it with my audience.

The video absolutely flopped. On top of that, I received a handful of comments from longtime subscribers who expressed extreme disappointment in my work, leaving remarks such as, "This is not up to the mark. You can do better videos and better content than this." To be honest, I was pretty bummed about the whole experience. I didn't realize I held myself to a certain standard because deep down, I still struggled with the lie that I needed to be perfect to be loved. It was clear that the Lord wanted me to confront those lies once and for all. If I had failed at a makeover just five years earlier, I would have felt too discouraged and ashamed to even share the video because I didn't have the emotional resilience to bear the critique. At this point in my life, though, I had built the mental fortitude I needed to seek purpose in what seemed to be a setback.

As I was beginning to reflect on my own heart, I came across a long, heartfelt message in my DMs from a woman named Renee,** who wrote:

> Great Powder Room video and just the message I needed for today. Exhausted from trying and trying only to run into obstacles and blocks. This coming Wednesday the 15th, I'll have to spend my first night sleeping in my car. I'm terrified but cannot afford housing anymore. Last night I decided I'd clean my apartment out, find someone to adopt my sweet dog, then end my life sometime this weekend. This morning I saw your YouTube video and then started looking up videos of people living safely in their cars and how they get showers, food, etc. It made the process look more manageable. I'm still scared, but willing to at least try. Thank you for your positive messages. The Lord's really using you! Please keep me in your prayers.

I immediately responded to Renee and thanked her for her vulnerability. After getting to know her more, I found out that we led strikingly parallel lives: we were both raised by single mothers, our fathers are both in heaven; we had a brush with homelessness; we served on a worship team; and more. In the YouTube video of my testimony, I shared my experience of being committed to a psych unit, and my story had resonated with Renee when she saw it. It was a strange feeling learning of someone whose life was so similar to mine and yet whose current reality looked completely different.

** "Renee" (pseud.).

I also learned she had been living in an additional dwelling unit (ADU) that had been illegally built by her landlord. The city found out and threatened to demolish it that week, leaving her with nowhere to live. She was currently working for Meals on Wheels, which delivers meals to senior citizens, but it didn't provide enough compensation for sufficient housing in her area.

Renee's story struck a chord in me. I remember what it was like to feel abandoned and ashamed of myself, as though I was a burden to my loved ones and society. I remember the panic of not knowing where I would sleep the next night and questioning whether life was worth fighting for. Sometimes a person can follow all the right steps and do all the right things, and life will still throw curveballs their way. I knew that better than anyone. So for the first time ever, I took the initiative to create a GoFundMe for Renee. I didn't know how effective it would be, but I knew I had to try. The more I talked to her, the more I understood why God had interrupted my filming to teach me a lesson on how to let go and trust him amid roadblocks and uncertainties. God took control of my calendar and changed my message entirely just to reach that one person. Renee was the one sheep for whom Jesus had left the ninety-nine.

To my surprise, the GoFundMe hit $8,000 in its first week and surpassed its goal of $10,000 by the second week. At the end of the fundraiser, my online community had donated a total of $15,257 to help Renee find housing while she got back on her feet. This was enough to sustain her for at least the next six months!

I had never felt more purposeful than when I mobilized my influence in that way. Throughout the process, Renee continually expressed her gratitude for the abundance of kind prayers, comments, and donations. She said, "Nervous as each day goes by, but feeling far more hopeful and, honestly, accountable to my donors to stay alive and keep trying. Accountability can be a strong, life-saving force!" Renee expressed that even though the money was important, it was truly secondary to the overwhelming demonstration of generosity that covered her in her most frightening moment. God met her where she was and used a small creator on YouTube like me to show his lavish love to her at just the right time. Our heavenly Father made use of our sufferings and didn't let our tears go to waste. My roadblocks allowed me to help Renee, and Renee's story will serve to help countless others.

Perhaps the most astounding demonstration of God's love is seen in his willingness to get messy, endure the suffering with us, and then turn things around in his perfect timing. God has always been in the business of using for good what the enemy meant for evil. I love Psalm 56:8, which reads, "You keep track of all my sorrows. You have collected all my tears in your bottle. You have recorded each one in your book."

This is the kind of heavenly Father who created us—one who pays close attention to what hurts us because it hurts him too. Yet he still chooses to endure the suffering with us because he knows that on the other side of our pain is tremendous purpose. Don't worry if your current reality doesn't seem to align with the promises of God. Allow yourself to trust in God each day, and witness how he redeems your purpose by using your unique story to impact the lives of many.

> **You prepare a table before me**
>> **in the presence of my enemies.**
> **You anoint my head with oil;**
>> **my cup overflows.**
> **Surely your goodness and love will**
>> **follow me**
>> **all the days of my life,**
> **and I will dwell in the house of the LORD**
>> **forever.**
>
> **PSALM 23:5–6 NIV**

Just for You

Take a deep breath and allow yourself to fully absorb all you've learned. When you're ready, take a few moments to reflect on the prompts below.

1. Do you feel like you have a firm grasp on your spiritual, physical, and vocational purposes?
2. Which layer of purpose do you struggle with the most, and why?
3. Name one thing you can do in this season to strengthen your sense of purpose.

Let's Pray Together

Dear heavenly Father, thank you for your daily guidance and provision in my life. I may not be where I want to be, but I trust that I'm exactly where I need to be right now. Thank you for walking alongside me. I pray that you will give me clearer vision for my next steps. Although I don't know all the answers, one thing I'm certain of is that I want to live a life that brings you great glory. Thank you for allowing me to participate in your mighty plans. Please continue to guide me in how to live a life worthy of the calling I have received. In Jesus' name. Amen.

Section 2

Framing

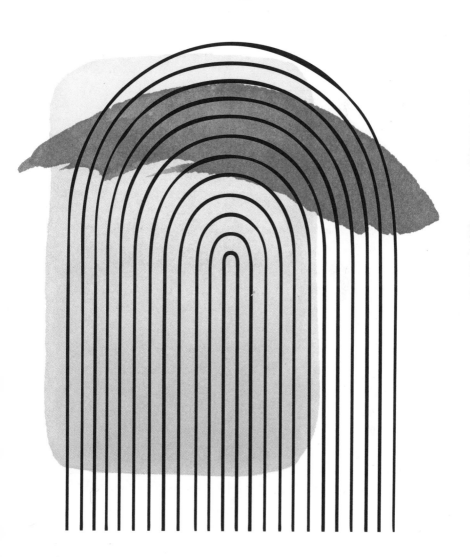

*I*n March 2021, my husband and I purchased a large, 1940s fixer-upper in his hometown. It had glossy red hardwood flooring and pale yellow walls. There was a pink bathtub with moldy jets, a fireplace that didn't work, and a termite-eaten back patio. Despite the atrocities, we knew the house had good bones and fell in love with its potential. When we began demolition, that was when I realized the critical importance of framing.

Part of our lofty ambition to renovate the entire home was to have the construction crew tear out a load-bearing wall in the kitchen to turn it into an open floor plan. The load-bearing wall was supporting most of the weight of the second floor, so if the wall were to be demolished, the ceiling would need to be reinforced to prevent a collapse. It was not reinforced.

I remember nonchalantly walking into the kitchen to check out the renovation progress and seeing a hairline crack on the first support beam, then a larger crack on the second, and a finger-sized crack on the third. By the seventh beam, the ceiling was sagging from the weight of the second story. I panicked and called the construction crew to come back that same day. A worker took one glance at the sagging ceiling, widened his eyes, and whistled. Thankfully, they were willing to build a makeshift frame in place of the previous load-bearing wall to hold up the ceiling. The flimsy two-by-fours bent slightly under the weight, but it was still better than nothing at all. A few days later, under the guidance of a structural engineer, the team installed an enormous, 17-inch-thick block of solid wood to hold up the second story properly. The cracks were finally mended.

If we had left the space frameless for even a week longer, the second story likely would've collapsed. It wasn't designed to hold itself up under that much pressure without any support. Think of the last time you felt like pieces of your life were under this kind of immense pressure. It's normal to feel pressure from time to time, but we only break down when there is no infrastructure to keep us up, or when the infrastructure is poorly designed. The way my ceiling started sagging is exactly how *we* tend to respond to a lack of structure. Now that you've learned how to build a solid foundation on Christ's love, find your safe people, and discover your purpose in him, the next step is to reinforce your new life with the proper framing to uphold it.

Just like the construction of a house, the process of framing takes a *lot* of heavy lifting. You will encounter weights you never knew you were carrying and discover vulnerable areas you've left unattended for a dangerous amount of time. It takes a great measure of intentionality and consistency to build strong framing for your life, but the payoff will be worth it. With proper framing, you can live an enduring and abundant life free from the fear that everything will one day come crashing down. When the storms of life hit, you can rest assured that the emotional infrastructure you've built will keep you standing firm and steady.

We are pressed on every side by troubles, but we are not crushed. We are perplexed, but not driven to despair. We are hunted down, but never abandoned by God. We get knocked down, but we are not destroyed.

2 CORINTHIANS 4:8–9

Chapter 6

Strengthening
Your Boundaries

*Those who don't take responsibility for
their lives remain stuck because they
want other people to change. . . . This
is the essence of powerlessness.*

Dr. Henry Cloud, *Changes That Heal*

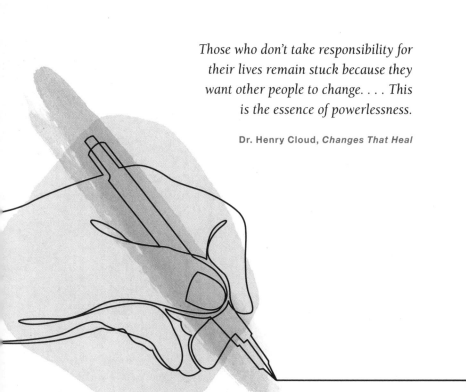

*F*raming is a tough and laborious job, but once you put in the effort, your forever home will begin to take form. Framing is the bare bones of the boundaries between what should be inside your home and what should remain outside. It is the structure that brings clarity, protection, and safety to your home. Likewise, when you build proper boundaries for your life and maintain them, you will have the internal framework to keep yourself whole and secure during difficult seasons and relationships. You will also be freed to voice your needs without fearing loss of love. And most of all, you will discover your true value as a human being apart from the critical opinions of others.

The first time I was explicitly taught about boundaries was by my Christian therapist. While it seemed that everyone I knew took pity on my mother and sided with Wendell, my therapist was the first to suggest I might benefit from moving out of my mother's house and finding a different church. At the time, I thought that leaving my mother's house was an act of disobedience, and leaving church an act of disloyalty (and perhaps even blasphemy). Still, I became more open to her advice as I grew to trust her little by little. I still remember her reaction when I told her I saved enough money to properly move out of my mother's house. She let out a faint smile of relief, straightened up in her chair, exhaled, and proceeded to teach me the most important lesson about boundaries.

"Imagine you're a mouse and your mother is a cat," she said. My cheeks reddened with shame at the thought of framing my mother as a predator, but I just said, "Okay." She continued,

"Up until now, she's been chasing you around a pole. What do you think would happen if you suddenly halted?" I stared at her blankly. "The cat would slam right into you, right?" she asked. "Yep," I answered, still not understanding where this was going. She said, "You and your mom have been in a frustrating pattern of disconnection and abuse for years, so now that you're putting a stop to it once and for all, she probably won't accept it quietly. There might be some real pushback, but if you don't stop it now, you'll always be stuck in the same loop with her."

I nodded and kept this metaphor in the back of my mind. Sure enough, my mother wailed and threw a tantrum when I gently told her I would be moving out. Though it was uncomfortable to refrain from apologizing profusely or giving in to her tantrum, I kept reminding myself of the cat-and-mouse metaphor and stuck with my decision.

To this day, this remains the healthiest decision I've made on behalf of both of us. It was the first time I had drawn a clear boundary with my mother and upheld it consistently. No matter how many family members guilt-tripped me for letting my single mother live alone or how many phone calls I received about my mother's attention-seeking crises, I maintained my boundary and never moved back. I found other ways to accommodate her needs and fulfill my duties as a loving daughter, such as surprising her with an early retirement years later and helping her out with her bills, but I kept my word to maintain a healthy physical distance between us.

Because of this clear boundary, we are now the healthiest we've ever been as individuals and as mother and daughter. Despite her initial protest, my mother now loves the peace of having her own space and the new routine she has established. She no longer has to worry about working for her survival, but actually makes time to take care of herself daily. Her unexplained body aches dissipated and her stress-induced migraines went away. She looks years younger than before and has a much more positive outlook on life.

Likewise, I've been able to thrive without the constant relational stress holding me back. I can create a home that truly feels safe and stable, all the while growing into my own person and discovering my likes and dislikes outside of my mother's influence. I discovered that I'm quite the introvert rather than the extroverted loudmouth I thought I was my entire life. I discovered that it was okay to genuinely like being feminine, and that leaning into my femininity does not make me vain or shameful. Most importantly, I learned that what my mother thinks about me does not have to dictate what I think about myself. I learned to love the person I've grown to become, despite the critical voices of others.

People tend to believe that the more comfortable you are with someone, the fewer boundaries should be drawn, but that couldn't be further from the truth. The closer you are with someone, the more you should be intentional about maintaining proper boundaries so that the relationship can continue to thrive in love and respect. Boundaries can help us salvage our mental health and the health of our most important relationships.

The Limits of Pain

One of my favorite books on this topic is *Boundaries* by Drs. Henry Cloud and John Townsend. The authors explain that healthy boundaries are not walls, but rather fences.[1] Walls tend to trap everything on the inside, whereas fences can be opened and closed based on your discernment. Like fences, healthy boundaries can let the good in and keep the bad out. Creating boundaries allows you to know where *you* end and another person begins.

Think of property lines—they define what belongs to us and

what belongs to another person. We are each responsible for our own thoughts, feelings, and actions. These are the things within our property line. How another person thinks, feels, or acts is within their property line and is therefore *their* responsibility. Without distinct boundary lines, we'll experience resentment, confusion, and a lack of ownership over our lives. At their core, boundaries create the infrastructure for a sustainable relationship with ourselves and the people around us.

While I was living with my mother, no clear boundaries were ever drawn between us. She could slam my door open during all hours of the day, rip open my mail before giving it to me, and generally be as intrusive as she pleased. Likewise, I was free to behave rudely in return, stay out with my friends for days, and bring home whomever I wanted without checking in with her first.

There were no rules, only unspoken bitterness and resentment. We didn't know how to communicate when our boundaries were crossed because we weren't aware that such a thing existed. We also didn't know how to clearly communicate our needs, only how to react explosively when our unspoken needs weren't met. Rather than owning our reactions and toxic behaviors, we were owned *by* them.

Thankfully, the repetitive pain and stress of our dysfunctional relationship finally pushed me to seek professional help, and I was able to draw the proverbial line in the sand. As Cloud and Townsend explain, "We change our behavior when the pain of staying the same becomes greater than the pain of changing."[2] In my case, the pain really was a blessing because it pushed me to acknowledge my limits.

Setting that first boundary with my mother was heartbreaking, but the cat-and-mouse chase was truly unbearable. We should not judge or ignore the stress we experience around certain people; rather, it should make us curious about our feelings.

Lean into them. The anxiety you feel around certain people may very well be a signal that your limits are being pushed or that a boundary is being crossed.

In a way, your feelings of anger and resentment can be helpful because they mean that your "boundaries radar" is working. Your brain is alerting you that someone is crossing your property line without your permission, and it's causing you pain and discomfort. Now, it is *your* responsibility to speak up, communicate your boundaries clearly, and commit to a consequence you are willing to live with.

For me, the consequences I had to accept when I moved out of my mother's house included a possible tantrum from her, gossip from my family members, and years of guilting and shaming from my loved ones thereafter. Sure enough, all of these things happened, but I had already built the mental and emotional fortitude to accept them. Seeing my predictions come true actually gave me a sense of relief because it confirmed that real change was coming.

Building an Internal Framework

When you first erect boundaries, it may seem harsh—almost like punishment—to the other person. However, boundaries are not about punishment, but protection. It is about giving people the right amount of access to you. Think back on the idea of your life being within the bounds of your property lines. If a stranger approaches your home, you may want to keep them outside your fence. If they prove to be safe, you may invite them to your doorstep. If they become a friend, you may invite them into your living room for a cup of tea. If they become a close friend, you may even give them a tour of your entire house.

The same idea applies to your relational boundaries. Not everyone deserves access to the most intimate parts of your

Boundaries

are about giving people

the right amount of

access to you.

home immediately. If you would not trust a stranger to roam your house, you should not give an untrustworthy person disproportionate access to your life. Because you are the rightful homeowner, you can choose whom to invite over and whose access you may need to revoke.

You may learn with practice that those who respect your boundaries will encourage separateness and accept your nos. Those who don't respect your boundaries will show you love only when you're compliant. Pay close attention to how you feel around the people in your life, and practice saying no first to those whom you deem safe. For me, I first practiced setting boundaries with my therapist. She would typically ask me to do a mental body scan to see how I felt around a certain topic or traumatic memory. If something was becoming too disturbing to talk about, she would create a safe space for me to say no and talk about something else. She was never impatient or nosy, never pried past my limits, and never treated me any differently, no matter what I chose to do. She was the surrogate attachment figure I needed to set boundaries with the unsafe people in my life.

In his book *Changes That Heal*, Dr. Henry Cloud tells a story about a woman named Jane who found herself unable to leave an abusive relationship. Reading Jane's story was like reading my own. Every nuanced torment she had endured and every cocktail of emotions she had experienced felt familiar to me:

> She was in a double bind that many abused people find themselves in. They literally "can't live with him, and they can't live without him." They can't live with him because of the abuse, and they can't live without him because of the isolation. Jane learned a crucial lesson: There must be internal bonding for one to be able to establish boundaries. Without it, boundaries as they were meant to be cannot exist. It is limits without love, and that is hell.[3]

Setting limits against an unsafe person without a strong sense of self-worth can be even more daunting than enduring the abuse to begin with. Remember how my ceiling sagged when we removed the load-bearing wall? The ceiling caved in under its own weight because it didn't have the internal support to uphold it. By practicing setting boundaries with a trustworthy friend, you build resilience against the backlash you might receive from unsafe people. My relationship with my therapist helped me create the internal infrastructure and emotional security I needed to maintain my boundaries when facing protest.

When we enact boundaries with people who are used to crossing them, one thing is almost guaranteed: they will be upset. They are accustomed to roaming our properties and redecorating our homes without our permission, so if they feel like their access has been revoked, they will be hurt. You may feel an urge to do away with your boundaries to console them, but remember that your boundaries are not for punishment, but protection. They are intended to protect your energy levels, emotional capacity, and sense of security, but they also protect your relationships with others. If someone doesn't know your house rules, they cannot abide by them. As the rightful homeowner, you must lay out clear rules for what you allow or disallow in your life. Your rules may upset your guests, but it is not your job to regulate their emotions for them. If they come into your home and respect your house rules, they may be a guest you would gladly invite over again. However, if they disrespect your house rules, the best thing you can do to guard your heart against bitterness and resentment is to revoke their level of access to your life. Creating limits for boundary-less people is like creating structure for children. They may grieve the loss of freedom, but structure will keep them and everyone else safe in the long run.

Dealing with a hurt family member or a dear friend is delicate and painful, but just remember that your boundaries are good for them too. Enabling them or even rescuing them from the natural consequences of their actions robs them of their ability to be responsible for themselves. In the book of Proverbs, the writer shares this wisdom on setting boundaries: "Hot-tempered people must pay the penalty. If you rescue them once, you will have to do it again" (Proverbs 19:19). True biblical boundaries lead to loving people despite their imperfections, not rescuing people from the consequences of their actions. As much as we want to, we cannot enable people into repentance.

When my mother finally adjusted to the structure I had set, I witnessed her reclaiming her sense of independence. She learned to enjoy her own company and began to rely on her peers for emotional support rather than only on me. Without my nudging, she had even managed to open a gym membership on her own! She now swims every day, making friends with the other swimmers at the pool and going out for group dinners with them. Her outlook on Jesus has evolved as well. She used to view salvation as a merit-based gift and often used the name of Jesus in condemning contexts. Now she speaks a lot more about his goodness and grace. She prays out of an overflow of gratitude rather than fear or anxiety. Indeed, she is the happiest I've ever seen her—all because I finally made the decision to stop enabling her codependency, her overreliance on me. The limits I had set for our relationship freed her to build the internal framing for her own life apart from me.

The eventual reconciliation I experienced with my mother is not necessarily a common occurrence. Some people never adjust to boundaries at all. I did not set boundaries with my mother because I wanted to change her; I set boundaries so I could protect my own peace of mind. Whether or not she was willing to respect my boundaries was completely out of my control. If we set boundaries as an attempt to change people, we will most likely be left disappointed. Boundaries are not for punishment or manipulation, but for our own protection.

Dwelling, Grace, and Truth

When we set boundaries with others in grace and truth, we reflect the essence of God's character. God is a boundary-full God. By nature, God is love, and his unconditional love is a perfect blend of grace and truth. His truth gives us direction, structure, and wisdom, and his grace frees us to be true to ourselves without fear of condemnation for our mistakes. Both grace and truth are needed to create a safe and sustainable relationship, a peaceful dwelling for our souls.

The Ten Commandments are a clear example of God's truth. As a loving Father, he gave ten clear rules for his children to follow to protect us, help us exist in harmony, and ultimately love each other well. Not many people would willingly admit to liking rules and regulation, but these guardrails provide us with a sense of safety, clarity, and direction. We can thrive in the safety of these guardrails, given that we already feel secure in God's love for us. Truth is a necessary ingredient to love; otherwise, we will run the risk of hurting ourselves *and* our relationships out of ignorance.

The ultimate example of grace is what Jesus did for us on the cross. Notice that because God is holy and just, he did not let sin be swept under the cosmic carpet. Instead, he bore the punishment for our sins on himself so that we can truly be cleared of our trespasses. Showing God's grace in relationships does not look like rescuing people from the consequences of their actions but rather like acknowledging their wrongdoings and forgiving them in our hearts. We bring glory to the Father when we can set clear boundaries with our loved ones while working on forgiving them in our hearts for their trespasses. When truth is expressed in the context of grace, it produces clarity, structure, and order— things that ultimately protect our peace of mind and strengthen our relationships.

When I made the decision to move out of my mother's house, my plan was not to abandon her or cut off our relationship altogether. Some relationships might be too dangerous to grant access to our lives, but I felt like ours just needed some space for grace. My prayer at the time was that God would continue to work on our hearts so that we could experience reconciliation one day.

So while I did create physical distance between us, I did not withdraw my love. I loved my mother from afar by praying for her daily, and when I discerned it was safe to approach her, I visited her house to share a meal with her. If she said something I didn't appreciate or did something I felt was inappropriate (for example, sending me photos of deceased family members in open coffins as a way to express her grief), I gently told her I didn't appreciate it and to please stop doing it. I had to clearly communicate that if she continued to say or do inappropriate things, it would make me too stressed to interact with her often. These were not empty threats but rather the communication of clear boundaries. I made sure to commit to each consequence I set. She always pushed back at first, but because I remained true to my word, she eventually started to respect my boundaries.

I showed my love for my mother in this way for a few years before I saved enough money to offer to pay for her bills and give her an early retirement—a gift that truly touched her heart and gave her both financial and relational security. Although my boundaries might have broken her heart at first and forced her to face her fear of abandonment, my firm communication reassured her that I still loved and cherished her. It slowly became clear to my mother that my boundaries were meant to protect both of us. As each year passes, she continues to become more secure in both my love for her and God's provision in her life. Our newfound boundaries took our mother-daughter relationship to a whole new level. There is now so much more understanding, empathy, and stability between us. Our lives are no longer shaken by misunderstandings, and we are free to live in true peace and security.

Truth without grace is, as Henry Cloud puts it, hell.[4] It is limits without love, justice without mercy, and rules without relationship. A relationship that is filled with truth and devoid of grace is grounds for rebellion. On the other hand, grace without truth is enabling. It is not really love at all because it aims to rescue others at the cost of our own needs. If we extend grace alone without the structure of truth, we run the risk of resenting the other person. Love should not lead us to resentment. Understanding God's boundaries in the context of his love helped me extend these loving boundaries to my mother. Truth and grace together will help us build the framework for a safe and peaceful home we would want to call ours forever.

I will show you what it's like when someone comes to me, listens to my teaching, and then follows it. It is like a person building a house who digs deep and lays the foundation on solid rock. When the floodwaters rise and break against that house, it stands firm because it is well built.

LUKE 6:47–48

Just for You

Friend, now is the time to pause and reflect on all you have learned. When you are ready, consider the questions below.

1. In which areas have you established the strongest boundaries?
2. Have you thought about limiting someone's involvement in your life?
3. How can you practice establishing healthy boundaries this week?

Let's Pray Together

Dear heavenly Father, thank you for modeling what it looks like to communicate clear boundaries in an honest and loving way. Thank you for providing me with structure and clarity on how to live a life that is pleasing to you. I pray that you will strengthen my resolve when it comes to communicating healthy boundaries with the people in my life. Like Jesus, I want to love people wholeheartedly while still preserving the integrity of who I am. Please give me the courage and comfort to do that. In Jesus' name. Amen.

Chapter 7

Shielded by Grace

Truly he is my rock and my salvation;
he is my fortress, I will never be shaken.

Psalm 62:2 NIV

*M*any of us carry an enormous weight from all the hurt we have experienced. Even if we're aware of the weight and long for it to be gone, the trauma doesn't always fade with time. In many cases, we relive the effects of the pain we've endured as though it is happening in real time.

We want our lives to be upheld by strong bones that can carry us through the most chaotic seasons. When my ceiling was sagging under its own weight and my contractors gave it a temporary fix with flimsy planks of wood, the wood began bending under the tremendous pressure. That kind of framing only creates more liability and is *not* the kind of framing you want for your forever home. Strong framing must be calculated for the amount of weight it needs to carry in order to provide true protection. Since the weight of the trauma doesn't usually change, the only thing that can change is our internal framework. This is where divine protection makes a difference.

Generational Trauma

A year before writing this book, Jon and I had an incident at a boba shop. We were in charge of grabbing twenty-six cups of boba for our Young Adults ministry, but the boba shop was unexpectedly packed that evening. What should have taken twenty minutes ended up pushing close to forty-five minutes past our Young Adults meeting time. As the minutes painstakingly passed by, the tension between me and Jon grew unbearable. At first, he paced back and forth impatiently. Then after a half hour, he couldn't contain his frustration any longer and began to vocalize it, most of which was directed toward me.

Both of us were anxiously waiting for our drinks with a horde of other people surrounding us. I felt physically and relationally trapped—a huge trigger for my anxiety attacks. I managed to contain my anger and anxiety until we got into the car. My hands began shaking uncontrollably, my legs grew numb, and my heart was practically beating out of my chest. Jon had already gotten most of his frustration out of his system, but I was having a full-blown anxiety attack.

It was clear that my body was reacting to a much deeper threat; one of being trapped in a dangerous relational conflict that rendered me powerless. I couldn't think straight. It was a visceral reminder of what it was like to have my prefrontal cortex shut down by trauma. My body was flooded with adrenaline and was ready to fight or flee. Pieces of my therapy sessions suddenly came to mind. I remembered my therapist saying, "If your reaction isn't proportionate to the situation at hand, then you're reacting to something in the past." It was a sign that my window of tolerance wasn't as wide as I had thought. The window of tolerance is the space where you feel comfortable and can handle the stressors of everyday life. For those who have been traumatized, our windows of tolerance are much narrower, which means we blow up or shut down faster than others when we are overwhelmed. I was no longer within my window of tolerance.

I hurriedly dropped Jon off at the gathering and drove back to our apartment, trying to calm myself down along the way with all sorts of breathing exercises. Not having Jon in the same space helped a lot, but by this point, my brain had already spiraled down a dangerous path of escaping. Please note that I didn't necessarily want to die; I just desperately wanted to get away because I felt unbearably trapped. Not every person who has suicidal ideations actually wants to experience the pain of dying; they just cannot bear the pain of being alive and are desperate to make it stop. It is a deep and urgent sense of panic that can only be relieved by the thought of not being alive anymore.

In the safety of my car, I googled the keywords "painless ways to go." It wasn't my proudest moment, but it was a trauma response and an experience I needed to have. To my surprise, the first result to pop up was the National Suicide Prevention Lifeline. This was before the 988 number was rolled out, so I had to tap on the clumsy call option and wait for a human voice to come through. This was the first time I had ever contacted any sort of suicide hotline, so I didn't know what to expect. A staticky elevator song suddenly blared through my speakers, snapping me back into the present for just a moment. The inappropriately happy music actually felt pretty grounding, and my heart rate slowed down. It went on for what seemed like a minute, which is an eternity to someone who thinks they are on their last leg. Then the music was interrupted by a long automated message, followed by a few more seconds of ringing before the empathetic voice of a young woman finally came through. By the time I spoke to her, I had already calmed down considerably.

"Hi there, may I ask what caused you to reach out to us tonight?" she asked. I told her I was having an anxiety attack and couldn't help but want to end my life. She listened to my story and gave the occasional "Mm-hmm" and "Uh-huh" to let me know she was engaged. Then she gave me practical advice on how to calm my anxiety and reminded me of all the things I had to look forward to the next week. I followed her advice (listened to worship music, went for a drive, and watched my favorite shows on YouTube) and felt my senses return after a short while. I was glad I had called.

When Jon ubered back from Young Adults ministry, he gave me a tender hug and a sincere apology. It turned out that the topic of their meeting was about breaking unhelpful traditions—a timely topic for us, to say the least. He shared how his habit of blaming others came from a long line of witnessing his elders deflecting blame, and that he was determined to break this habit for the sake of our marriage.

After our sweet conversation, I realized that the tradition I clearly needed to break was the generational trauma I had inherited. My mother suffered from anxiety attacks, as had my grandfather and his father before him. God came through for us that evening by bringing our problems to light while making sure we knew he had our best interests at heart. Through the painfulness of our fight and the gut-wrenching panic of my anxiety attack, God made it clear that the unhelpful traditions of our past still had power over us. What might have helped us survive in the past was hijacking our peace in the present.

The Armor of God

God's protection began with naming the problem, but he didn't stop there. The very next day, which was Valentine's Day, two separate friends sent me this passage from the book of Ephesians. The section was aptly titled "The Armor of God":

> Finally, be strong in the Lord and in his mighty power. Put on the full armor of God, so that you can take your stand against the devil's schemes. For our struggle is not against flesh and blood, but against the rulers, against the authorities, against the powers of this dark world and against the spiritual forces of evil in the heavenly realms. Therefore put on the full armor of God, so that when the day of evil comes, you may be able to stand your ground, and after you have done everything, to stand. Stand firm then, with the belt of truth buckled around your waist, with the breastplate of righteousness in place, and with your feet fitted with the readiness that comes from the

gospel of peace. In addition to all this, take up the shield of faith, with which you can extinguish all the flaming arrows of the evil one. Take the helmet of salvation and the sword of the Spirit, which is the word of God.

And pray in the Spirit on all occasions with all kinds of prayers and requests. With this in mind, be alert and always keep on praying for all the Lord's people.

Ephesians 6:10–18 NIV

This passage is well-known because of its empowering metaphor of divine protection. The apostle Paul reminded the church in Ephesus that their struggles were "not against flesh and blood, but against the rulers, against the authorities, against the powers of this dark world and against the spiritual forces of evil in the heavenly realms" (6:12 NIV) In other words, he warned them not to view their problems as mere physical adversities, but to be aware of the political, moral, and spiritual battles lying underneath. Paul was directly addressing spiritual warfare.

Notice that all but one of the pieces of the armor of God are defensive in nature: the belt of truth to hold the armor together, the breastplate of righteousness to guard our hearts, the shoes of readiness to keep us standing firm, the shield of faith to protect us from direct attacks, and the helmet of salvation to safeguard our minds against the lies of the enemy. The only offensive weapon is the sword of the Spirit, "which is the word of God" (6:17 NIV).

When I received this empowering passage from two of my friends the day after my suicidal ideation, it confirmed that the Lord wanted to protect me. He did not condemn me for my attempt to escape and dissociate, nor did he leave me to fight this battle on my own. Instead, he shed light on the unhelpful traditions that still had a foothold in my life, helped me and Jon to reconcile, and then sent two messengers to remind me that his divine protection was still available. All I had to do was put on his armor and equip myself with his Word, which keeps me standing firm "when the day of evil comes" (6:13 NIV).

Underneath our discouragement, chaos, and fear is usually an unresolved hurt. For me, I was reacting to a much deeper trauma than simply my fight with Jon in the boba shop. The spiritual warfare I was battling against was the generational trauma that caused my anxiety attacks. The part of my brain that senses danger, the amygdala, was now programmed to sense danger in even the subtlest conflicts. I mean, I ideated about suicide over boba. That's a prime example of a trauma response if I've ever seen one.

Once my amygdala got activated, my prefrontal cortex quickly shut down and my body immediately prepared to fight or flee. Everything becomes heightened when you are traumatized. This is just the kind of struggle the enemy loves to exploit. Thankfully, the battle was not mine to fight on my own.

Have you ever wondered why the term is "spiritual warfare"? Warfare indicates that there are two opposing forces. One is a clear enemy that wages war against your soul, but the other opposing force isn't you; it is the Lord. You are not left to fight on your own. In Christ, you have access to his divine protection. You can truly be safe at the deepest, most sacred level—your soul. With the full armor of God protecting you from the external spiritual warfare, you can feel safe enough to focus on rebuilding your internal framework.

Reprocessing One Frame at a Time

That anxiety attack confirmed that my internal framework wasn't as strong as I had thought. The extent of knowledge I had about trauma and the brain made little difference to my nervous system. As soon as a trigger presented itself, I reacted in the same way as before—shaking, throwing things, screaming, and then going into full, suicidal shutdown mode. Certainly these were extreme reactions to harmless triggers that felt completely out of my control. After I received the spiritual support I needed from the Lord, I was once again empowered to seek out ways to rebuild my mental resilience, one frame at a time.

I began reading about a form of trauma therapy called eye movement desensitization and reprocessing (EMDR). The success stories that came from this type of treatment caught my attention. Studies suggest that EMDR can be even more effective than cognitive behavioral therapy for patients with major depression and PTSD and is a powerful treatment alternative if PTSD medication doesn't work.[1]

EMDR is a form of treatment that has been around since 1948 and was founded by a woman named Francine Shapiro. Shapiro was taking a stroll through a park to shake off some negative thoughts when she noticed that darting her eyes back and forth reduced the intensity of her anguish. She wrote:

> While walking one day, I noticed that some disturbing thoughts I was having suddenly disappeared. I also noticed that when I brought those thoughts back into mind, they were not as upsetting or as valid as before . . .
>
> Fascinated, I started paying attention to what was going on. I noticed that when disturbing thoughts came into my mind, my eyes spontaneously started moving very rapidly back and forth in an upward diagonal. Again the thoughts disappeared, and when I brought them back to mind, their negative charge was greatly reduced. At that point I started making the eye movements deliberately while concentrating on a variety of disturbing thoughts and memories, and I found that these thoughts also disappeared and lost their charge. My interest grew as I began to see the potential benefits of this effect.[2]

Through further research, Shapiro discovered that eye movements dramatically improved symptoms of PTSD, such as intrusive thoughts, depression, anxiety, and flashbacks. When her patients' eye movement was stimulated, they were able to revisit traumatic memories without a complete shutdown of their prefrontal cortex. The prefrontal cortex is responsible for our reasoning, creativity, imagination, and the ability to tell the difference between the past, present, and future. It shuts down when we are in survival mode to help us focus on fighting or fleeing from the source of danger.

Sadly, traumatized people always feel as though they are in danger. The trauma has rewired our brains to be extra sensitive to potential triggers, which means that our prefrontal cortexes are rarely at ease for a long period of time. The past is constantly relived in the present because our ability to tell time literally shuts down in the face of potential threats or intrusive flashbacks. The traumatic memory does not get filed away as a thing of the past but continues to cycle in an ever-present loop of anger, fear, resentment, and pain.

However, when Shapiro's PTSD patients revisited their traumatic memories during EMDR, their prefrontal cortex remained activated. EMDR stimulated both brain hemispheres to help their subconscious minds file away traumatic memories as part of the past.[3] Today, this therapy uses a variety of audio, visual, and kinetic tools to re-create this bilateral stimulation.

Psychologist Bessel van der Kolk noted that there could be a connection between the effects of EMDR and what happens to our brains during REM sleep. He explained, "The eyes move rapidly back and forth in REM sleep, just as they do in EMDR. Increasing our time in REM sleep reduces depression, while the less REM sleep we get, the more likely we are to become depressed."[4]

He goes on to suggest that it's because of the eye movements that our prefrontal cortex remains activated, as it is during REM sleep. This activation allows those with PTSD to reprocess their traumatic memories with a new perspective because more of their brain is involved, which can give them a healing sense of closure that traumatized victims seldom experience. Dr. van der Kolk also made an observation on the effects of medication on his patients versus the effects of EMDR:

> Drugs can blunt the images and sensations of terror, but they remain embedded in the mind and body. In contrast with the subjects who improved on Prozac—whose memories were merely blunted, not integrated as an event that happened in the past, and still caused considerable anxiety—those who received EMDR no longer experienced the distinct imprints of the trauma: It had become a story of a terrible event that had happened a long time ago. As one of my patients said, making a dismissive hand gesture: "It's over."[5]

According to van der Kolk, many of his PTSD patients reported feeling that their trauma was a thing of the past after EMDR. Though it remains an unpleasant memory, it no longer rears its ugly head in their lives with the same level of intensity and immediacy. There can now be a cognitive distance between their present lives and their traumatic past.

After my deep research on EMDR, I bit the bullet and gave it a try. I found a highly rated clinic just down the block from where I lived, and I invested several months into receiving this treatment. The first two months were dedicated to history taking and resourcing:

- taking record of my life story
- exploring traumatic memories
- identifying present triggers

- creating future goals
- equipping myself with self-soothing tools in preparation for EMDR sessions

My new therapist, Cathy,* asked if I had any specific memories that I wanted to reprocess. I suddenly thought of the time when I went on a trip to San Francisco with my mother when I was nine.

"Do you want to discuss it in detail or just keep it in mind during our EMDR sessions later on?" she asked. Apparently, you don't even need to vocalize your traumatic stories for EMDR to work! This therapy relies mostly on your brain's ability to reprocess memories as a thing of the past rather than on the usual talk therapy. After consideration, I chose to tell her the story in detail because it was comforting to talk about this with someone I trusted.

The story began when my family moved into a tiny additional dwelling unit (ADU) when I turned nine years old. This was only a year after my mother had recovered from a life-threatening car accident that caused broken ribs, damaged organs, and multiple hemorrhages in her brain. The doctors had told us we should prepare for her funeral arrangements, giving her just a 5 percent chance of survival. That week, my mother's friend came to visit her in the ICU while she was in a coma, and her friend whispered, "You can't just die. You have to stay alive to raise Anh. Otherwise, she will be motherless." My mother teared up in her coma, and from that day forward, she exceeded everyone's expectations and achieved a miraculous turnaround.

When we had moved into our new ADU, it was more than just another relocation; it signified hope, healing, and change. Yet it was clear to both me and my father that my mother wouldn't go unscathed from the accident. Her mental state was never the

---

* "Cathy" (pseud.).

same after her brain surgery. She was much more prone to dysregulation and violence—mostly toward my father. Some of the worst fights they ever had were in that house, and this particular one was the worst of all.

One day, my mother asked me, "Do you want to come with me to San Francisco to visit Aunt Hoang?" I shouted, "Yes!" I looked forward to that trip all week. It was the first trip I had taken with just my mom. I couldn't wait to have fun with her. She told me all about what to expect in San Francisco and all the amazing foods we'd be able to sample. When the day came, I was so excited that I grabbed my own luggage and ran ahead of her to climb onto the bus.

When we arrived in SF, we were picked up by an older man whom I didn't recognize. He was friendly, so I just assumed he was my mother's friend. He drove us to his house and then grabbed our luggage out of the trunk. I asked, "Where is Aunt Hoang?" He and my mother looked at each other and burst out laughing. "I *am* Aunt Hoang!" he snorted. My mother said, "Just call him Aunt Hoang, okay? He likes that name." I felt slightly uncomfortable but didn't know what to think of it, so I complied.

The only other time I felt disturbed during the trip was when he wanted my mother to sleep in his bedroom, but I protested because I didn't want to sleep by myself in a stranger's house. Besides that, I was taken to all of the famous tourist spots and was babysat by his older son for the rest of the time. It wasn't a bad trip; it just felt novel and quirky.

When we arrived back home, my mother took one step through the front door, dropped her luggage, and made a bee-line toward my father in the bedroom. She repeatedly screamed, "What did you do?" while stomping on the floor and punching her sides with her fists. I remember being stunned at how quickly she exploded from zero to 100. I just stood there sobbing and feeling terribly helpless.

I only heard bits and pieces from their fight, but that day I learned that my mother had used me to legitimize her trip to have an affair. I also learned that my father had been cheating on her as well, and that this was her way of seeking revenge after finding out. So to retaliate, my father spent their life savings on random furniture and gambling. There was so much chaos in their yelling match that I couldn't even comprehend what was happening.

At one point, I ran between them to try to help them make peace. I tried to force a smile through streams of tears and snot and told my father that we had only hung out with a person named Aunt Hoang in San Francisco and that he had nothing to worry about. His face took on the most tender expression I'd ever seen as he patted my head and said, "It's okay, honey. Ba isn't mad at you. Just stay in the room, okay?" After that, they moved into the living room and fought violently.

The fight reached a point of no return when my mother grabbed my father by his hair, threw him down before our family altar, and made him confess his sins to Jesus, Mary, and my late grandmother. My father complied, and I felt the sting of his humiliation. Halfway through, he came to his senses and stood up against my mother. He got angrier and angrier until my mother ran into the bedroom where I was hiding, punched herself repeatedly, and then called the cops on my father. The cops arrived within minutes and arrested my father for a crime he had not committed.

I stopped at this point in the story and said to my therapist, "I don't know what that memory taught me or why it's significant, other than the fact that it was disturbing, but I keep having flashbacks about it. I just have trouble seeing how it affects me today."

Cathy said, "Well, how did you feel when you were in that room?"

I said, "Mostly scared and sad. I just wanted them to stop fighting."

"It sounds like you must have felt really trapped and helpless too."

When she said the word *trapped*, something clicked. I realized that I usually utter that word right before I'm neck-deep in an anxiety attack. "I'm trapped" was a very clear, unhelpful belief that I held. It was the root cause of my desperate desire to escape whenever I sensed relational conflict, and why I went so far as to entertain suicidal thoughts during the boba incident. When I was hiding in that bedroom at nine years old, I *was* literally trapped. There was nowhere else I could go to seek shelter from all the yelling and screaming. "I think being trapped is exactly it," I said. "That feeling terrifies me and makes me want to escape. I just can't bear it."

She replied, "Well, then, we can start with this memory."

The Altar of Protection

Cathy gave me the option of experiencing the traditional finger movements or her preference—hand buzzers. I chose the hand buzzers because the idea of keeping my eyes open during these intense memories seemed too distracting. Cathy reached into her tote bag for what looked like a pair of tangled earphones. She scooted her couch closer to mine, carefully untangled the buzzers, and placed one in each of my palms. "They're meant to give the same bilateral stimulation as the eye movements without all the extra visual distractions," she said. After adjusting herself in her chair, she continued, "I'm going to start the buzzers slowly at first so you can get familiar with how they feel." I nodded. The buzzers started, and they actually didn't feel too bad. The slow, interchanging pulsations were quite cathartic.

She said, "Now I'll set the buzzers at the speed we'll use during reprocessing. It's going to be faster because it's meant to activate your nervous system." The buzzers pulsated quickly like a thumping heart in each of my palms. We repeated this a couple of times while practicing the tools I had learned, such as the self-soothe container and calming visualization. I've included both exercises in the back pages of this book to help you experience them yourself.

Then our session began.

Cathy started the buzzers at the quicker rate and reminded me of the key scenes from the San Francisco memory. She gently invited me to close my eyes and said, "Take yourself back to that time when you were nine years old and living in the one-bedroom house. You were hiding in the bedroom and your parents were fighting in the other room. Remember what it was like to feel trapped and helpless." It took a while for my mind to focus on that memory, but after a couple of minutes, I saw it in detail—my parents towering over me, screaming at each other like feral dogs. I was yelling for them to stop, but no one could hear me.

About thirty seconds passed, and Cathy said, "I'm going to pause the buzzers. Now take a deep breath. What do you notice?" I described the scene to her, and she said, "Hmm. Notice that. I'll start the buzzers again."

This time, I saw an even younger version of myself in that bedroom. I looked maybe six or seven years old, with a distinct bob haircut that made me look like Dora the Explorer. That little girl was sobbing uncontrollably, and I felt the whirlwind of sadness, confusion, fear, and disappointment inside her. It was a pitiful place to be in—not being able to remove herself from that chaotic environment. I felt a deep compassion for her.

Another thirty seconds passed, and the buzzers stopped again. We took a deep breath together, and she asked, "What do you notice?" Again, I described the scene and was reaffirmed before diving back in.

In the next frame, I walked toward my younger self, knelt down to her level, and embraced her. I could feel her tears wetting my shoulders and sense the anguish in her cries. I told her that the fighting would eventually stop and that she would have beautiful memories in that house too—that even though the situation was miserable, it wouldn't last forever. I could sense my younger self feeling more relieved but still deeply dreading that place. Even if the fight would eventually end, she would still have to ride it out in the meantime. The process was painful beyond what she could bear. I started crying with her while still embracing her.

The buzzers paused again, and we went through the same procedure.

I then saw the scene of that bedroom begin to fade, but the little girl was still sniffling by herself in the bedroom. I sensed her dread and couldn't bear to leave her by herself. I tried to will my mind to stay with that memory as long as I could, but the scene just kept zooming out slowly, like a drone shot. Soon my vantage point was from the living room. I still saw her sniffling in the bedroom and looking downcast, but something else caught my attention—the altar of Jesus that my mother had erected.

More pausing, taking deep breaths, reporting what had happened, and diving back into the scenes.

I maintained that same vantage point, with the little girl sniffling in the distance and the altar up close, to my right. I then sensed the Holy Spirit reassuring me that he was protecting her too. It made me feel like it was okay to leave that house (or that memory) because she would be in good hands. The Lord was there to care for her on my behalf.

Another pause and deep breath.

Something clicked in this next frame. It occurred to me that the altar in my living room, the one before which my mother used to condemn my father, was the same altar I saw in my mind's eye when I encountered Jesus in the back of the stranger's car. I sensed that God was telling me he had always been sovereign.

My mother might have misused the altar because of her struggles and insecurities, but Jesus didn't just see what she wanted him to see—my father's sins against her—he saw everything. He saw my father's broken heart, my mother's trauma, and the little girl who felt trapped in that forsaken environment. He saw it all, and he used the same image my parents had misused to save their daughter years later. I was overcome with gratitude and began to sob. It had all come full circle.

Cathy waited until the thirty seconds were up before checking how I was doing. I told her about the realization I'd just had, and how I had never noticed the significance of that altar until that moment. In just a couple of short sessions, EMDR loosened my mind to make the connections I otherwise wouldn't have made. I realized that God's protection had always been present in my life, no matter what my age or circumstance. It was such a deeply redemptive feeling to witness how Jesus was present in even my loneliest moments—to actually *see* his image in my old spaces of trauma and to inherently know he was sovereign over the situation. I was amazed by the kind of connections my brain could make when it was no longer in survival mode while thinking about a traumatic memory. Each frame I reprocessed through EMDR became a new building block for a stronger and more resilient framework for my life.

Real Security

In Pastor Rick Warren's bestseller *The Purpose Driven Life*, he wrote, "Real security can only be found in that which can never be taken from you—your relationship with God."[6] Many times, we can be deceived into deriving security from worldly things, such as finances, relationships, power, and influence. However, any sense of security that is derived from these things is ultimately distorted because these resources can be taken away from

While true love doesn't always *shield* us from pain, it equips us to *heal* the pain and turn it into *purpose.*

us at any point. The only enduring security is our relationship with the Lord, which can never be stolen from us or be compromised by our brokenness.

I learned from my EMDR sessions that real protection comes from having a relationship with the Lord himself. Real protection doesn't mean he will shield us from every pain and suffering life has to offer, but it does mean he will be with us through it all. This makes an enormous difference and equips the believer for a truly abundant life on earth.

I used to think the complete absence of pain would be better than having God by my side through the pain, but true love doesn't always shield us from pain. True love equips us to heal the pain and turn it into purpose. In other words, God's love fortifies our internal framework and strengthens our spiritual and mental resilience. He promises to redeem what the enemy meant for evil for our ultimate good and for the salvation of his people (see Genesis 50:20; Romans 8:28). As Timothy Keller wrote, "God will allow evil only to the degree that it brings about the very opposite of what it intends."[7]

To know that Jesus was there with me through the pain didn't erase or invalidate the suffering I went through, but it made it more tolerable and purposeful. This realization saved me from the anguish of feeling trapped whenever I sensed relational conflict, and it widened my window of tolerance against this kind of trigger. I no longer defaulted to a dissociative, suicidal state even when the trigger persisted. Because I know that God was in the trenches with me and had a plan for me all along, I finally have a grasp of real, divine security.

> **The LORD says, "I will rescue those**
> **who love me.**
> **I will protect those who trust in**
> **my name.**
> **When they call on me, I will answer;**
> **I will be with them in trouble.**
> **I will rescue and honor them."**
>
> **PSALM 91:14–15**

Just for You

Take a deep breath as you slowly absorb everything you have learned. Allow yourself the time and space to process it all. Once you're ready, reflect on the prompts below.

1. Which part of the "armor of God" section resonated with you the most (Ephesians 6:10–18)?
2. Reflect on a time when you saw God's redirection as a means of his protection.
3. Describe a time when you saw God bring redemption to a situation that seemed beyond repair.

Let's Pray Together

Dear heavenly Father, thank you for equipping me with your spiritual armor and shielding me with your grace. Please help me trust in your promises of redemption and restoration, even when I can't see the way forward. Give me a sense of peace and security in the knowledge that you are always with me, even in my darkest moments. Help me cling to the hope of Jesus and to remember that you will work in all things for my good and for your glory. Thank you for your unwavering love and for always being my place of refuge. In Jesus' name. Amen.

Chapter 8

The Power of Perspective

*Observing changes what occurs, but observing
also changes our perceptions of what occurs.*

**Shane Parrish's Farnam Street blog article,
"The Observer Effect: Seeing Is Changing"**

*D*id you know that your brain continuously modifies its structure and functionalities in direct response to your experiences? This is known as neuroplasticity. Even those who seem the most set in their ways have the capacity to change the way they think, no matter how difficult it may be. The brain can always be rewired to a certain extent, which is good news for trauma survivors.

I remember asking Cathy in the first few weeks of therapy if she thought there was any hope for me to truly rid myself of my triggers. She replied, "The brain is always capable of changing. Trauma changes the brain, but so does healing." Thus began my second journey with EMDR.

Trapped People Trap People

This time, we decided to revisit that same memory because it was still having an emotional impact on me. On a scale of 0 to 10, my distress level after thinking about the memory was still a 5 or 6. I dreaded revisiting that memory, but I knew that a one-hour session wasn't going to suddenly erase decades of chronic chaos and trauma. Cathy handed me the buzzers. I closed my eyes, and the session began.

Unlike the first time, my mind immediately took me back to the scene of chaos. I was observing my parents fighting as my present self, but my younger self was nowhere to be seen. I saw my father kneeling and sobbing at the altar while my mother was screaming obscenities at him. Then he slowly stood up, walked into the bedroom, and shut the door. This, of course, never actually happened. I knew at that moment that he would never come back out again. Then I was left alone with my mother in the living room.

At first, I felt a mixture of disappointment, sadness, and regret. I wished I could've stood up for my father before he left for good. My mother was standing next to me in awkward silence. I could sense that she was sad and regretful. Then a wave of anger came over me, and I said everything I've always wanted to say. "Why did you do that to him? How can you torture people like that? Why do you have to always seek revenge? Are you happy now?" These thoughts came out in overlapping waves of frustrations. My mother just stood there, looking guilty and indignant all at once. Then she ran out to the front porch and cried.

I followed her to the porch and attempted to console her. Nothing I said could calm her down. She was inconsolable, like an abandoned child. I reached out to touch her, but she quickly pulled away and continued sobbing. It was at that moment that a phrase entered my mind: *Trapped people trap people*. I let out an audible chuckle at the absurdity of the phrase, but it was a connection I had never made before. It finally occurred to me that the reason she often trapped her family in chaos was because she felt trapped herself. She was kicked out of her home at age fourteen by my vicious grandfather, suffered from a severe car accident that rendered her semi-brain-damaged, and was struggling profusely in a country that initially promised an abundance of opportunities. She had nowhere to go. Of course she felt trapped.

Knowing this about her doesn't erase the fact that she deeply hurt our family, but it did help me understand that her trauma response truly wasn't a personal attack on me or my father. It wasn't about us at all. Trapped people trap people because it's all they know to do; it's a trauma response they haven't yet worked through. Their reality continues to recycle the past over and over. I came to understand it wasn't my job to console her because her deep pain originated from a much older lineage than I could handle.

When I made sense of this in my mind, the scene on the porch suddenly faded to black with just me and my mother standing in the darkness. I could hear her sobbing even harder and saying, "Now I don't even have a porch to cry on!" Then I saw a bright white light in the distance. The light source came from a statue that looked like Christ. My mother didn't pay much attention to it; she just kept sobbing pitifully. The Christ figure came closer and closer until it was so large and bright that my mother couldn't help but stop crying and look up. Strangely enough, the Christ figure looked like an enormous 3D version of the Christ paintings you see on Roman Catholic candles. He was as tall as a skyscraper and looked quite silly from our viewing perspective.

My mother started giggling at the silliness of the Christ statue, and it made me feel so touched that I teared up. Nothing I did had been able to console her—not my words of affirmation, quality time, or physical touch. She was inconsolable. Yet she was now laughing freely like a child because Jesus was able to reach her in a way I couldn't. He distracted her from her pain using humor, and he restored the peace in her heart. He was the parent she needed—the one who could comfort her and heal her from her incredibly deep sorrows.

I came out of that session with a brand-new perspective on God's love. He showed me the creative ways he relentlessly pursues his children. In the book of Romans, the apostle Paul wrote, "Can anything ever separate us from Christ's love? Does it mean he no longer loves us if we have trouble or calamity, or are persecuted, or hungry, or destitute, or in danger, or threatened with death?" Paul continued, "No, despite all these things, overwhelming victory is ours through Christ, who loved us. And

I am convinced that nothing can ever separate us from God's love. Neither death nor life, neither angels nor demons, neither our fears for today nor our worries about tomorrow—not even the powers of hell can separate us from God's love" (Romans 8:35, 37–38).

Even though I lashed out at my mother in my mind, the Lord saw through my anger and understood my yearning for her to be whole again. He showed me that he was able to speak her language and console her in a way I could never even hope to do, which releases me from the pressure to be her savior. I was able to see my mother whole again, even for just a moment, and it gave me hope that one day she'd experience that peace and safety in real life. True to the Scriptures, neither our fears for today nor our worries for tomorrow can separate us from the love of God. His love covers all, and through reprocessing my traumatic memory, I was able to witness just how far he is willing to go to show us his unconditional love.

Remember that the reason traumatic memories elicit intense reactions in victims is that these memories have never been fully processed. The prefrontal cortex shuts down during traumatic events, so the victim remains trapped in the same traumatic loop indefinitely, causing them to relive the intensity of their trauma whenever a trigger is present. For their traumatic memories to be turned into normal memories, the traumatic memories must be updated or altered by their observation and reframing.

Let's look at ways to reframe your perspective on your traumatic memories.

Becoming the Observer

Perhaps a reason treatments such as EMDR and different types of mind-body therapy methods (aka somatic therapy) are so effective for healing trauma is that they utilize something similar to the observer effect. In physics, the observer effect is the phenomenon in which the mere observation of something eventually changes the thing itself, even if by a tiny fraction.[1] When it comes to revisiting traumatic memories through EMDR, the person is able to become an observer of their experiences rather than having their prefrontal cortex shut down by the traumatic memory itself (as in the case of flashbacks or triggered reactions). This act of observation allows the brain to discover new perspectives it couldn't see before. We must be able to observe our traumatic memories in a safe environment with our prefrontal cortex activated to successfully work through them. The trauma will lose its power over us when we can reprocess those memories and reframe them in a way that leaves us feeling empowered.

Dr. Peter Levine, the developer of the Somatic Experiencing therapy, said, "When a memory is revisited, you have a period of some hours afterwards when a new memory is reinstalled. And that new memory becomes now the real memory, the true memory." He continued, "The thing about *traumatic* memories is that they don't change. The thing about healthy memories is that they're constantly being updated."[2] The lack of updated perspectives causes the painful memory to stay unresolved, even for years after it first happened.

The cognitive bias known as the framing effect states that a person's decision is influenced by the context in which the information is given.[3] For example, a child is more likely to get upset to hear that their bag of candy is "almost half empty" rather than "halfway full." Similarly, many of us are more likely to buy a product that claims it kills 99 percent of bacteria rather than claiming only 1 percent of bacteria will survive. The way things are framed makes a difference in our choices, emotions, and behaviors because our brains are quick to evaluate risks and losses.

Since a "glass half empty" mentality may hinder us from

enjoying life as it was intended, here is how we can take advantage of the "glass half full" perspective.

How to Reframe

First and foremost, reframing should happen in the presence of a trained therapist or mental health professional. In addition to EMDR, other therapies such as IFS (internal family systems), CBT (cognitive behavioral therapy), and a wide range of somatic therapy methods listed in the back of the book can provide new perspectives on trauma. In my experience, it is counterproductive to reframe by yourself or with a friend if you or your friend are unfamiliar with ways to recover from trauma. Reframing walks a fine line between restructuring our thoughts and gaslighting ourselves, which leads us to deny our painful experiences to feign a more favorable reality. We cannot deny the painfulness to a body that bears the truth.

Let's look at six other practical ways to prepare our minds for reframing, in addition to seeking mental health care:

1. **Ground yourself in Scripture.** I believe that the Bible is the living and breathing Word of God and that it has the power to help you battle negative thoughts. You can start by journaling about your disruptive thoughts, identifying the underlying fear, and then searching Scripture to see what the Lord has to say about that fear. Most of the time, the act of reading Scripture on its own is already quite grounding. It puts me at ease and allows me to think more clearly. More often than not, I end my devotional and Bible reading time with much more clarity and calmness than when I started. In addition to the grounding aspect of reading the Bible, the wisdom it provides helps anchor us in the truth of God's love.

2. **Get educated on trauma.** The more you understand the way the brain and the mind work, the easier it will be to reframe potential triggers and have empathy for yourself and others. By picking up this book and dedicating yourself to healing from your trauma, you are already making strides in your healing process. Mental health education can empower you to navigate your experiences in a gentler and more compassionate way.

3. **Interrupt your negative thought cycle.** This strategy can be more appropriately labeled as diverting rather than reframing, but it helps you get to a place where you're better able to change your thoughts. Before your brain starts spiraling downward, set measures in place to distract yourself from spiraling. For this strategy to work, you'll have to identify your triggers and come up with alternate options for your reaction. Anything that pushes you out of your window of tolerance and makes you feel anxious, angry, or irritable may qualify as a trigger. For example, if my trigger is relational conflict, I would make a list of helpful things to do immediately after anxiety hits—things such as listening to worship music, walking my dog, or reading at a café. This list would remind me that I have other ways to respond to my trigger than to spiral down the familiar path of negative thinking. By interrupting your negative thoughts with a grounding activity, you give yourself the chance to revisit the situation later on when you are in a calmer state of mind. Successful reframing can only happen when you feel safe.

4. **Investigate your fears.** Rather than catastrophizing or letting your anxious thoughts linger, start fact-checking your fears. Ask questions such as, "Can I actually guarantee that the worst is going to happen?" and "What evidence do I have to support that this fear-producing thing will

happen?" By fact-checking yourself, you're also interrupting your negative thought patterns, giving yourself the chance to empathize with your fears, and grounding those fears in reality. In rare cases where fact-checking actually makes your fears worse, remind yourself that there is a spectrum to the truth. Ask, "Is this way of thinking helping me?" Just because a thought contains some truth does not necessarily make it productive or beneficial.

5. **Befriend yourself.** A great way to reframe your negative self-talk is to think, *Would I say this to a friend?* If that thought is too mean to bear, remember that you should speak to yourself just as kindly as you speak to others. How you speak to yourself matters because it shapes your self-worth, the way you behave, and the choices you make. People with a greater sense of self-worth and self-respect tend to make healthier decisions for themselves than those who don't see their own self-worth and speak to themselves poorly. Be a gentle friend to yourself, for you are the only one who will ever inhabit your own experiences.

6. **Focus on the good.** I've heard it said, "When you focus on the good, the good gets better." If the process of reframing could be summed up in one particular quote, this would be the one. By magnifying the good, you will start to notice all the other good things you have to look forward to. When you feel triggered, the pain may cause you to feel hopeless, as though you'll never again enjoy the things that once made you happy. In survival mode, the only thing that matters is escaping from the point of danger, so finding the good or the positive meaning in things won't be the easiest task. This is why I highly recommend speaking to a mental health professional or even getting in contact with one of the services listed in

the back of the book if you have a hard time reframing your destructive thoughts.

Reframing Your Suffering

An existential problem that many traumatized believers struggle to reframe is the problem of suffering: if God is all-good, then why do evil and suffering exist? Timothy Keller proposes a meaningful outcome of suffering:

> You will never really understand your heart when things are going well. It is only when things go badly that you can see it truly. And that's because it is only when suffering comes that you realize who is the true God and what are the false gods of your lives. Only the true God can go with you through that furnace and out to the other side. The other gods will abandon you in the furnace.[4]

What this excerpt means is that our experience of pain and suffering does not negate the goodness and unconditional love of God. The Scriptures remind us that *despite* our pain and suffering, we can still have overwhelming victory in Christ. Keller surmises that the significance of our suffering is, at least in part, that it teaches us to discern between the real God and our false idols—the temporary things we seek security from in place of God. Reframing suffering in this way helps us extract meaning from our traumatic experiences without betraying our sense of logic. The point of reframing is never to replace negative thoughts with empty, positive thoughts, but rather to replace them with realistic thoughts—thoughts that truly make sense to us in light of what we know about God and the world. Only then can we genuinely be empowered by our new perspective.

Suffering teaches us to discern between the real *God* and our false *idols.*

God can be good and still allow us to suffer in order to bring us closer to himself. There are numerous theodicies—defenses of God—that have to do with the problem of evil, but if we're talking about the Christian God, then we must consider his relational nature. At his core, God is a loving Father. If we can accept that he is a loving Father, then any suffering we experience must be allowed for a good purpose and can be redeemed for the good of his people.

The scene of my inconsolable mother belly-laughing at the giant, silly Christ figure was the perfect embodiment of the questions the apostle Paul posed to the believers in Rome:

Can anything ever separate us from Christ's love? Does it mean he no longer loves us if we have trouble or calamity, or are persecuted, or hungry, or destitute, or in danger, or threatened with death? . . . No, despite all these things, overwhelming victory is ours through Christ, who loved us.

Romans 8:35, 37

My mother was, by all means, walking through the furnace. She was crying as though her entire world was on fire because, for many valid reasons, it was. She was first betrayed by her own flesh and blood and then betrayed again by the love of her life. But with God, she could still feel a measure of safety and have joy even in the midst of her suffering. That was the ultimate reframing I needed to witness firsthand.

Real Change Is Possible

The more you train your mind to reframe negative experiences in order to extract insight, purpose, or empowerment from your trauma, the easier it will be to make reframing a habit. Rebuilding your internal framework is not just wishful thinking, but it is a real possibility with the right help, education, and practice.

I pray that the Lord will continue to strengthen the framework of your life so that you will not be in despair but have genuine hope. Though you may have suffered for a while, may he restore, support, strengthen you, and place you on a firm foundation (see 1 Peter 5:10). In Jesus' name. Amen.

> **"I have told you all this so that you may have peace in me. Here on earth you will have many trials and sorrows. But take heart, because I have overcome the world."**
>
> **JOHN 16:33**

Friend, allow yourself to pause and take a deep breath as you reflect on everything you have learned. Give yourself the permission to process it at your own pace. Then when you're ready, consider the prompts below.

1. What negative thought pattern have you had trouble reframing?
2. Which of the six tips for shifting your thought patterns resonates with you the most?
3. How do you plan to practice reframing in this season of your life?

Let's Pray Together

Dear heavenly Father, I know that sometimes my own thoughts can lead me astray and cause me to doubt your goodness and faithfulness. Please help me to recognize when this is happening and then turn to you for guidance and comfort. Please give me the strength and courage to speak truth over my life, even when it's difficult. I trust that you will transform my way of thinking and renew my mind. Thank you for your unconditional love and for your constant presence in my life. In Jesus' name. Amen.

Chapter 9

Strategies for Endurance

While other worldviews lead us to sit in the midst of life's joys, foreseeing the coming sorrows, Christianity empowers its people to sit in the midst of this world's sorrows, tasting the coming joy.

Timothy Keller, *Walking with God through Pain and Suffering*

*W*hen our contractors rushed back to build the makeshift frame for our sagging ceiling, we all took a step back and looked carefully at the job, and they immediately knew to call for reinforcement without my nudging. The sheer gravity of the second story made the planks of wood look like a joke. There was no way that only three planks would be able to endure all that pressure. By the time the team of men were done, it looked like they had built enough framing to replace the previous load-bearing wall altogether! And that's exactly what it takes to endure for the long run:

1. **Ongoing assessment.** We must continually step back and reflect on the overarching goal so we can keep moving in the right direction. For example, I still go to therapy once a week to check where I am and what I may need to shift. If weekly therapy is outside of your budget at this time, you can opt for monthly or even quarterly check-ins with your therapist.

2. **Deliberate resolve.** We must continually remind ourselves of our ultimate concern so we can push through difficult seasons. I find it helpful to remind myself that God's love for me is the kind of love I want to show to those who have hurt me—love that is full of grace and truth.

3. **Reinforcement.** We must recruit adequate help and support along the way. It would've been nearly impossible for me to seek healing on my own without the help of anyone else. The African proverb rings true in this regard: "If you want to go fast, go alone. If you want to go far, go together."

Endurance is not always about enthusiasm; it's often more about maintenance. Lasting strength comes from regularly checking in with ourselves, acknowledging our emotions, and accepting the fact that we cannot navigate this marathon called life alone.

Angela Duckworth wrote in her bestseller *Grit*, "What we accomplish in the marathon of life depends tremendously on our grit—our passion and perseverance for long-term goals."[1] The passion and perseverance she mentions are the main ingredients for the development of resilience. Coincidentally, these are the exact same two ingredients that are most affected when we suffer from trauma. As I mentioned in earlier chapters, our sense of purpose gets diminished during traumatic episodes because our prefrontal cortex shuts down.

Perseverance without passion is like being in survival mode. We are not thriving when we are persevering; we are simply trying to stay alive. Yet passion without perseverance is like a fleeting flame that will quickly die out. Only by combining the spark of passion with the grit of perseverance can we ignite a fire that will burn brightly and guide us through even the toughest challenges.

Ongoing Assessment

Just as pilots must regularly check their instruments to ensure they're on the right course, we too must pause and assess our lives to make sure we're heading in the direction we want to go in. If we remain on autopilot, we may find ourselves veering off track.

Most of my adolescence was spent chasing after the next high—achievements, substances, relationships—just about anything but God. When our flesh takes hold of us and we live under the tyranny of our urges, we set ourselves up for failure. By continually taking pauses, consulting with the Lord, and reevaluating the state of our hearts, we can prevent mental, emotional, and spiritual burnout. Such burnout narrows our window of tolerance, making us feel the burdens of our trauma all the more. The best way to boost our mental, emotional, and spiritual endurance is to build intentional time for reflection into our daily schedule.

Let's look at three practical steps we can take to build this life-giving habit:

1. **Choose a cue.** Use an existing, repetitive cue in your daily life to remind yourself to have a reflection time. This can be the view of the sunset, your phone alarm, or even brushing your teeth. Find a daily cue so that the routine you're going to set will fit naturally into the rhythm of your day.

2. **Set a routine.** Once you have your cue, prepare a routine that works for you—going for a walk in the park, writing in your favorite journal, reading the Scriptures in your cozy nook, and so forth. Create a routine of reflection that you can genuinely look forward to each day.

3. **Enjoy the reward.** Ensure that your routine is followed by a natural reward—something tangible like a hot bath or a warm cup of tea, or something intangible, like the satisfaction of completing another journal entry or the peace you feel after spending time with the Lord. Whatever it may be, your reflection time won't become a habit unless there's a clear reward each time. Thankfully, spending time with the Lord will always yield a measure of mental, emotional, and spiritual payoff.

When we reflect prayerfully, we allow the Holy Spirit to speak into our lives and remind us of our "why"—our overall purpose or ultimate concern. This goal will hold us accountable on the path we need to walk as people who strive for endurance, healing, and Christlikeness.

Deliberate Resolve

The researcher of grit and endurance Angela Duckworth says on her website, "Grit is about having what some researchers call an 'ultimate concern'—a goal you care about so much that it organizes and gives meaning to almost everything you do. And grit is holding steadfast to that goal. Even when you fall down. Even when you screw up. Even when progress toward that goal is halting or slow."[2]

What is your ultimate concern? Is it to bring purpose out of your pain? Or to glorify your heavenly Father? Whatever it is, you must clearly identify your ultimate concern so that you can keep going back to that worthy goal when life becomes painful. As for me, my ultimate concern is to share the sweetness of God's character with everyone I know.

I've noticed a different part of God's character resonating with each person he touches, and that is the chief characteristic his followers usually preach the most. I was most touched by how sweet God is as a Father, so I dedicated my ministry to conveying his sweetness to those who are hurting. This ultimate concern helps me realign my heart when I'm tempted to not be kind or gentle to others.

In the book of Romans, the apostle Paul wrote, "We can rejoice, too, when we run into problems and trials, for we know that they help us develop endurance. And endurance develops strength of character, and character strengthens our confident hope of salvation" (Romans 5:3–4). Paul's ultimate concern was to strengthen his hope in the Lord. He was so resolute about this that he was able to withstand—even rejoice in the face of— adversity, because it gave him the opportunity to strengthen his endurance and pursue his ultimate concern. True to his word, Paul demonstrated his spiritual tenacity by writing multiple letters to the churches in Ephesus, Philippi, and Colossae while suffering in prison. Because he deliberately resolved to trust in the Lord, he endured through the suffering and made an eternal impact on the Christian church.

According to Paul, we can choose to rejoice even in the face of adversities because "they help us develop endurance." Endurance, then, strengthens our character, and character "strengthens our confident hope of salvation." In other words, trials become opportunities to develop our endurance. When we strengthen our endurance, we can become more resilient, confident, and faithful in our relationship with God.

Rick and Kay Warren have demonstrated this Pauline endurance. The couple have been pioneers of the suburban megachurch for more than forty years, and Pastor Rick himself has written one of the most widely translated books in the world, *The Purpose Driven Life*. Beyond their achievements and accolades, what impressed me most about the Warrens was the way they persevered through the most tragic moment in their lives.

Pastor Rick and Kay's youngest son, Matthew, was known to be a particularly kind, gentle, and compassionate man in his community. "He had a brilliant intellect and a gift for sensing who was most in pain or most uncomfortable in a room," Pastor Rick lovingly shared. "He'd then make a beeline to that person to engage and encourage them."[3] Matthew spent much of his time in the quiet quarters of the church's Resources Warehouse, where he looked after the inventory of books and DVDs. It was a low-key, service-oriented job that suited his kind temperament.

Matthew's closest friends and family knew he couldn't always show up as the positive and playful person he was at his core. Matthew struggled with borderline personality disorder and severe depression throughout his life. One day, after spending a fun and lighthearted evening with his parents, Matthew went back to his home in Mission Viejo, battled a severe episode of depression through the night, and in the morning ended his own life.

I still remember the exact moment I heard this news blaring on my TV that Sunday morning. This event shook the entire Christian community. Up until then, discussions surrounding mental health were still taboo in both the church and secular culture. Matthew's passing sparked the most important mental health reevaluation I had ever witnessed in the Christian community. As for the Warrens, they suffered immensely but chose to endure. In an interview, Pastor Rick made these comments:

> The day that I had feared might happen one day, since he'd been born, and the day that I prayed would never happen, happened. And I remember, as we stood in the driveway, just embracing each other, and sobbing. And Kay was wearing a necklace—you're wearing it today—that had the words of a book she wrote a year ago called *Choose Joy*.
>
> And she held it up and it said, "Choose joy." And in my mind I thought, "Are you kidding? How can I choose joy in this worst circumstance of my life?" But we—even in that moment—we were trying to say, "We're not in control but we do have a greater hope and we do have a source of joy that isn't based on our circumstances." And it was a holy moment.[4]

Even in the most confusing and excruciating moment in their lives, the Warrens chose to hang on to the promise of joy. Pastor Rick later elaborated on this decision to choose joy. "You are not to rejoice in the problem. You are to rejoice in the Lord," he said. "God is not asking you to be a masochist. . . . God is not expecting you to put on a happy face and say, 'Everything's fine!' when it's not fine. That's lying. [The Bible] doesn't say give thanks *for* the problems in your life; it says to give thanks *in* all circumstances."[5] Indeed, the only reason the Warrens were able to look past their current sorrows to cling to the Lord was that they had practiced their resolve for more than fifty years until they faced the ultimate trial of their lives.

Kay Warren said, "We know that joy is still present. We know it because God is good and because we have spent the last fifty years of our lives putting our spiritual roots down deep into the rich soil of God's grace . . . and because of those roots that have gone deep into the soil of who God is, getting to know him, when troubles have come our way, we have been able to produce endurance, and hopefully character, and from that character, hope and joy."[6]

You see, resolve is not a momentary decision or a sudden force of human will, but rather a faithful, daily practice. Resolve is the result of the daily decision to trust that the Lord is good and that he loves you no matter how happy or sad your circumstances seem. When you deliberately practice trusting in God's goodness daily, your framework will be fortified to withstand the truly painful, gut-wrenching moments that put your endurance to the test.

Reinforcement

The final step to fortifying our endurance is to recruit adequate help and support along the way. Ideally, people should be a part of our restoration journey at every phase. Seeking reinforcement is not a sign of weakness, but rather a sign of maturity, openness, and strength. We were not meant to endure through the hardships of life alone. The Bible says, "Carry each other's burdens, and in this way you will fulfill the law of Christ" (Galatians 6:2 NIV). In order to fulfill God's will for our lives, we must share our burdens with one another and lean on each other for love and support.

Many traumatized people struggle to ask for help when they need it the most because they fear vulnerability, but if this is you

Seeking reinforcement is not a sign of *weakness,* but rather a sign of maturity, openness, and *strength.*

today, I encourage you to challenge this fear. Practice asking for help with "safe people" first—people you trust and feel at peace around. Safe people will respect your boundaries and consistently show up for you when you need them. This can be your therapist or mental health counselor, a trusted friend, or members of your small group at church. When your safe community consistently demonstrates their love and support, it will empower you to weather the storms and stay hopeful for the future.

As pioneers of suburban church growth, the Warrens developed a system of small groups to help their megachurch feel more connected. People gathered at homes to share meals, catch up on one another's lives, study the Word, and pray for one another. These small groups proved essential for Rick and Kay's own spiritual and emotional endurance after Matthew's passing. In their first media interview after the incident, Pastor Rick said:

> I was overwhelmed by the love of our people. Kay and I had given 33 years to this church. And I felt like they all gave it back at the moment. It was just a very tender moment for me as a pastor. I have walked through the valley of the shadow of death with thousands of people. I have walked, I've stood at bedsides and seen lots of people take their last breath. I have been there for those people for 33 years. And they were there for us when we needed them most.[7]

Though they had all the reasons in the world to isolate themselves from their community after such an overwhelming and devastating event, the Warrens instead welcomed the support of their loved ones and graciously received their ministry of presence. They allowed the people they had served for thirty-three years to serve *them* in their most vulnerable season, and this openness facilitated further healing, bonding, and overall resilience.

During that time of mourning, Pastor Rick developed a sermon series titled "How to Get Through What You're Going Through." People were on the edge of their seats waiting to hear what *The Purpose Driven Life* author had to say about moving forward from his tremendous grief. It was to be the first sermon series after the very public death of their son, when millions of Christians were questioning how mental health might fit into the fabric of their faith.

Rick and Kay shared a hug onstage, and in the most daring display of authenticity, the couple relayed exactly what had happened in their faith journey during the sixteen weeks after their son's passing. The grieving mother said, "So what am I left with if I'm not going to blame God and I'm not going to blame myself? Where do we go with these dashed hopes? Well, what I'm left with is mystery. Big, fat mystery." She continued, "I don't know the answers . . . but I'm content to leave [the questions] there, because I know that the day I meet God face-to-face, every single one of those mysteries will be solved."[8]

It was a beautiful and raw recounting of their decision to trust in God's goodness despite their circumstances, and it brought empathy and hope to the hundreds of thousands of people who were watching and grieving in their own way. The Warrens showed how we don't have to know all the answers to endure, and that gave all who were watching the courage to adopt such a profound level of faith.

> **So let's not get tired of doing what is good. At just the right time we will reap a harvest of blessing if we don't give up.**
>
> **GALATIANS 6:9**

Just for You

Now is the time to take a moment and slowly digest everything you've learned. When you're ready, explore the questions below.

1. Which part of this chapter resonated with you the most, and why?
2. Are you more inclined toward passion or perseverance?
3. Which of the three strategies for endurance will you put into practice this week?

Let's Pray Together

Dear heavenly Father, thank you for being my source of strength when I'm at my weakest. I'm grateful that I get to lean on you when I'm exhausted or beaten down by life. Please help me to develop resilience and perseverance when facing the obstacles that come my way. I pray that you will surround me with like-minded people who love you—people who will spur me on to live a fulfilling life that is pleasing to you. I ask for a legacy that declares your power and goodness in my life. Though the storms will come, I want to learn how to weather them with you. In Jesus' name. Amen.

Section 3

Inspections

*W*hen a friend asked Jon and me how much we had agreed to pay our contractors for our home renovation, we reluctantly whispered the amount. They let out a gasp and told us about their connection with someone who could do anything we wanted for a third of the cost—*one-third*! With that much money saved, we'd be able to furnish our home as soon as we moved in. We could even have a new bed frame and sofa right away instead of sleeping on the ground while we worked to replenish our funds.

It was a tempting offer, but in true risk-averse fashion, Jon wrapped his arm around my waist to bring me back to reality. This one gentle nudge reminded me of our previous discussion about the three key values we wanted in our contractors: integrity, experience, and legal compliance. It was extremely important to us that whoever we worked with would not bypass the city code to get us what we wanted. The contractor recommended by our friend would have, more likely than not, delivered the *appearance* of what we wanted but at the cost of cutting corners on materials and sidestepping city inspections.

When we got home that evening, Jon said, "It's a good thing we didn't go with someone cheaper. Cheaper doesn't always mean better. We're not building a house just for looks; we're building it for our future children—and if anything were to happen to them because we avoided inspections, I wouldn't be able to live with myself." All my residual feelings of missing out were instantly replaced by relief and gratitude. It's amazing how quickly we can appreciate the proper path when it turns out that the shortcut is paved with trouble.

This same temptation to take shortcuts is warned against by Paul in his first letter to the Corinthians, where he used the analogy of building a temple to symbolize the building of one's walk with Christ: "Remember, there is only one foundation, the one already laid: Jesus Christ," he wrote (1 Corinthians 3:11 MSG). The beauty of being God's living and breathing temple is that we get to build our lives on top of what Christ has already done.

After accepting his unconditional love for us, we then must "take particular care in picking out [our] building materials" (1 Corinthians 3:12 MSG). This speaks to the internal framing of our lives—the enduring structures that will protect and support us in the long run. "Eventually," Paul went on to say, "there is going to be an inspection. If you use cheap or inferior materials, you'll be found out. The inspection will be thorough and rigorous. You won't get by with a thing" (3:13 MSG).

Imagine yourself walking into the construction site of your newly built life, with all the new habits and boundaries you've created by applying what you've learned in the first two sections of this book. You notice that the foundation of your new house has a solid core of concrete, with a cornerstone that symbolizes Christ himself. You step onto the foundation and run your hand across the cornerstone, taking in its strength and sturdiness. The cornerstone gives you the confidence that your new home will be fully supported, no matter what storms may come. You now make your way into what will become the family room, surrounded by the new wooden framing that shapes the structure of your house. You notice a feeling of safety in this fortified structure. The robust framing provides a clear boundary between what you want in your new home and what should remain outside.

You then notice the blue and red wiring laid out between the walls like the exposed nervous system of the house. Before the drywall gets installed and the tiles grouted, this is the time to make a final inspection. If you ignore the inspection process, what would have been easier to fix now will later become a problem. This is the time for you to inspect your inner progress so the destructive parts of your life don't get buried behind the walls and finishing touches later.

The beauty of being in Christ is that we will always receive a second chance at refining our framework and foundation, even if they don't pass inspection the first hundred rounds. This is also known as progressive sanctification—the process through which we learn to be more like Christ. It's a lifelong journey toward wholeness and holiness, one we can actively participate in through our daily surrender to God. This is a matter of reinforcing the integrity of our love, boundaries, and resilience so that we can truly reflect the heart of God and live like Jesus. Carrying out self-inspection through the lens of God's love ultimately results in our good. Conducting a grace-filled, loving introspection allows us to continue building a safe and stable home that will withstand troubles that come our way.

Let's be honest, no one likes inspections. To be examined under a magnifying glass for flaws and defects sounds like a terrifying experience, because it is. I remember how our contractors toiled for months to *ensure* that they would pass the inspections. Once or twice they had to go back and make minor tweaks, and their crestfallen faces said it all. Yet each time they *did* pass, their eyes lit up with pride and confidence in the integrity of their work. As their clients, we became increasingly grateful toward the inspectors as more serious matters were at stake. Even though the inspectors delayed our project by weeks at a time, we wouldn't have felt nearly as safe in our home as we do now without their wise judgment and expertise.

Inspections aren't meant to be fun, and they can even delay your plans longer than you'd like, but a well-inspected life will always be more steadfast than one that uses cheap materials and is riddled with shortcuts. The more you value the inspection process, the wiser and more prudent you'll become.

As you stand amid the beautiful new structure you've built for your life—with all the new framing fortifying your boundaries and the foundation of love that fuels your resolve, now is the time to take a pause, appreciate the work you've done, and run it through an inspection. May this be a lifelong guide to glean from, one milestone at a time.

Dear brothers and sisters, when troubles of any kind come your way, consider it an opportunity for great joy. For you know that when your faith is tested, your endurance has a chance to grow.

JAMES 1:2-3

Chapter 10

Embracing Full
Ownership

It's hard to own what you don't choose.

Lysa TerKeurst, *Good
Boundaries and Goodbyes*

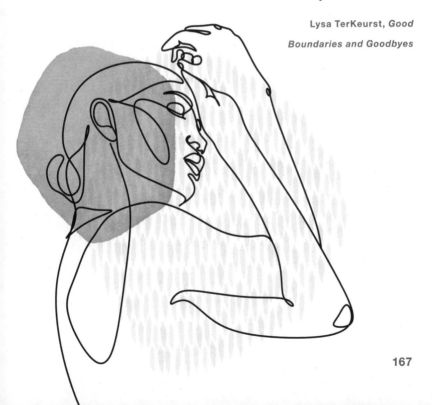

A fundamental part of the inspection process is taking action to mend the faults and defects that have been discovered. It's usually during this stage when people get a fuller picture of what it's like to be a homeowner. When you rent other people's properties, maintenance is just a phone call away. If the stovetop stops working, all you have to do is call the property manager and they'll have someone come to look at the gas line the next day. But when *you're* the homeowner, no one is responsible for the problems except you. Ownership of one's life can feel like an equally daunting task, if not an even *more* overwhelming experience than actual homeownership.

Owning Our Emotions

When I mention ownership, I mean the literal and emotional embodiment of our lives—letting ourselves fully experience the beauty, enjoyment, and responsibility of all that life entails. The problem is that trauma can impact our sense of ownership in a multitude of ways. In previous chapters, we learned that people can dissociate (or psychologically disconnect) from their body and environment in order to survive. We all need a healthy measure of dissociation to cope with the daily stressors of life— daydreaming, escaping through a novel, or even watching TV. Dissociation isn't always a bad thing. However, it becomes problematic when it gets in the way of our relationships, devotion to God, and daily responsibilities. Some people can be in a state of dissociation for years and not even know it. They can feel detached from their physical bodies, as well as from their sense of who they are and who God is. We can't skip the pain to get to the healing; we must feel it to heal it.

My journey of self-inspection deepened after marriage. I quickly found out that my self-abandonment tendencies were never fully resolved but only repressed. The very relationship I thought would usher me into healing suddenly became the stressor that made me dissociate from my own life. Even as I continued to post my peaceful devotional videos on YouTube, our first year of marriage was riddled with conflict—a roller coaster of gratifying peaks and dreadful valleys.

During one of the worst mental breakdowns I had ever experienced, I was crouching in a fetal position behind an ottoman in our bedroom with my head folded into my knees. I felt that if I were to let go of my body, I would shatter into a million pieces. My brain was so overwhelmed that I began slipping in and out of consciousness, muttering random memories that flashed before me.

One memory was of me as a small child, possibly two or three years old, staring into the ceiling of our front porch in Vietnam. I remembered not being able to express myself with words but feeling extremely neglected and confused as to why I was there. That memory surfaced from the deepest parts of me and made my heart sink. I envisioned my current self being in that helpless position once again, staring into the ceiling of our old porch with all the knowledge of my life thereafter. I felt so small against the tremendous amount of loss, abuse, and neglect that was to come. Through tears, I whispered out loud, "I wish I had never been born." I had fought to repress these feelings of regret for so long, but at that moment, I finally uttered the truth that my body had held on to all these years. Then in present time, I heard Jon quietly sob from the other room. He must have sensed that my mind was slipping away.

I began dissociating severely, feeling an out-of-body experience as though I was floating away from myself. I begged God to bring me Home. *Please, I don't want to be here anymore. Please have mercy on me. Let me fade into darkness. Let me go Home with you.* But instead of seeing myself fading into the darkness, as I had earnestly prayed I would, I saw myself settling down into our living room sofa with the morning sunshine caressing my face. The sun felt warm, calm, and comforting on my skin. Everything went quiet when I envisioned this scene. I began to notice the weight of my body again, the slow pulsing in my hands, the labored breathing. I was no longer floating aimlessly, but felt grounded, weighted, and aware of myself.

I later learned in Cathy's office that this experience matched a somatic therapy tool called light visualization. With this therapy technique, the client is usually guided by their counselor to listen to the emotions lodged within their bodies using imagery. A common method is to visualize warm, pleasant light shining on yourself, much like what I was doing. At the time, I had no idea why I was doing this.

"I just need to sit in the sun, but it's going to be such a long night," I muttered. Then Jon said, "God is your light. You don't need to hide in darkness. You can come to him right now and sit in his light." He walked closer to me and said, "Before you went into the bedroom, I opened my Bible and read from the book of Isaiah." I heard him shuffling in his pocket for his phone. "It said, 'The people who walk in darkness will see a great light. For those who live in a land of deep darkness, a light will shine. You will enlarge the nation of Israel and its people will rejoice'" (Isaiah 9:2–3).

My husband spoke clarity into my heart. He helped me realize that the Lord himself had become my counselor when I begged him for mercy. Instead of leading me into eternal darkness, God had led me into the light—into the warmth of his embrace. The divine light that I envisioned grounded me from the inside out, filling me with gladness. I sobbed in gratitude for God's loving intervention.

That night, I felt a palpable sense of release. It was the first time I allowed myself to bring that regretful thought to Jesus without judging myself for it. The point wasn't that I was right *or* wrong in wishing I had never been born, but that I was finally able to come to terms with this repressed thought, despite my feelings of shame. Previously, I couldn't let myself be ungrateful or unappreciative in any way—even at the cost of denying my own trauma. I acknowledged all the opportunities and resources that God had given me and the sacrifices that my parents made on my behalf, so it was difficult to come to terms with my true feelings. But I learned that night that the only way out of emotional pain is through it. My efforts to repress my wounds caused me to want to abandon my life in a dissociative stupor. But God, in his infinite mercy, led me into his glorious light when I finally revealed to him my most vulnerable thoughts.

To fully own your life is to own your most challenging thoughts. I encourage you to lend an ear to your challenging thoughts without invalidating yourself, no matter how uncomfortable it may be at first. You then can bring your most vulnerable feelings to the Lord as an offering. When you call out to him for help, he will be faithful to show you compassion and mercy.

Losing What We Have for What We Lack

Another way in which trauma can lead people to abandon ownership of their lives is by putting them in constant alert mode. Rather than dissociating, those who struggle with anxiety are always on the lookout for danger. They are hypervigilant of their surroundings, often neglecting their physical needs in the process. If we live our lives constantly feeling like people or situations can become dangerous at any point, we won't remember to take care of ourselves very well. Most of our energy will go toward keeping ourselves alert and alive.

Among other anxious biblical characters, King Saul was notoriously hypervigilant during his reign. Out of his sheer anxiety and paranoia, he struck down eighty-five priests on the baseless suspicion that they had conspired against him (see 1 Samuel 22:6–23). Rather than pouring himself into being as good a king as he could be, he gave into his fears, spending the vast majority of his later years chasing after David, the next prophesied king. Saul's fear of losing power and the people's adoration led to his eventual downfall. He chased what he lacked rather than stewarding what he had.

Saul himself admitted, "I have sinned, for I have transgressed the commandment of the LORD and [the prophet Samuel's] words, because I feared the people and obeyed their voice" (1 Samuel 15:24 ESV). Saul's fear of the people's rejection caused him to reject God, so as a result, he wasted years of his reign fearing the loss of power rather than stewarding that power. It is the ultimate picture of the imposter syndrome. Saul was the God-appointed king, yet he behaved as though he was still fighting for the throne.

Saul's story serves as a powerful reminder that our external abundance cannot fix our internal depravity. Without addressing the root of our fears, external blessings will never be enough to protect us from the destructive power of our insecurities. As the first appointed king of Israel, King Saul had an abundant amount of material possessions, social influence, and political power. He was set up for success in every regard. Yet he rejected God's decrees and his identity as the appointed king of Israel. His story serves as a cautionary tale for those who search for lasting security outside of God.

What It Means to Embody

Whether your past hurts have caused you to dissociate, feel helpless, become hypervigilant, or a mixture of all three, remember that all of these responses are caused by deep, valid issues. In a sinless world where we were not burdened by trauma, we'd have no need to dissociate, be hypervigilant, or feel powerless. These are called trauma responses because they are exactly that—our natural reactions to the dangers that threaten our security and well-being.

You are the way you are because you had to survive, but now you have a framework and foundation in place to help you build a new way to live. Inspecting these responses keeps them from sabotaging all the renovation work you've done thus far.

In somatic psychology, the term *embodying* means being completely present with our body, thoughts, and actions. It is what happens when we apply these three mindfulness questions regularly:

1. **What am I thinking?** If bothersome thoughts are vying for your attention, write them down, show yourself compassion for thinking these thoughts, and then prayerfully bring them to the Lord.

2. **What am I feeling?** Our emotions are often warning signals of underlying issues, like smoke from a fire. If we avoid or condemn our emotions because they make us uncomfortable, our forever home will run the risk of eventually burning down. Identify all the feelings you're experiencing so that you can bring them into plain view. If you have trouble identifying your emotions, I've included an Emotions Word Bank in the back of the book to help you pinpoint how you feel. This word bank comes in handy for both me and my husband when we have trouble figuring out our emotions.

3. **What am I doing?** Notice how your body is feeling right now. Do you feel achiness or tightness anywhere? Are your shoulders rigid or relaxed? Notice the sensations in your body and identify whether they feel good, neutral, or bad. Then you can determine what to do to help your body feel better, such as going for a walk, eating lunch, or doing a quick stretch. Traumatized individuals often feel disconnected from their bodies, so practicing scanning your body for pain or tension each day will help us regain ownership of and compassion for our sacred temples.

The practice of mindfulness can be life-altering for those who have been disconnected from their own bodies, thoughts, and emotions. When they finally reconnect with themselves, they feel as though they have unlocked parts of themselves that have been exiled or estranged for years.

Once we *experience* full ownership of our lives, the rest of the *journey* can become significantly more *bearable.*

Once we finally experience full ownership of our lives—the good, bad, and ugly parts—the rest of the journey can become significantly more bearable. During the year my husband and I renovated our forever home, we lived in his sister's spare apartment in a neighboring city. Every other day, without fail, I'd make the short drive over to our new house to monitor its progress and come back elated at the slightest development. Each time I would see a new tile layout or cabinet installation, the sheer joy of progress would override any previous growing pains—because I knew this was to be my forever home, a place I had designed with love and intentionality. It was a future safe space for my family, one I wanted to be filled with love, laughter, and the presence of the Lord. Despite investing my entire life savings and an exorbitant amount of time and energy into this project, I felt in my bones that the end result would be more than worthwhile.

Do you currently feel as though the new life you're building is worth the effort and growing pains? If you don't, I can also empathize. There were parts of my renovation that made me want to yank out my hair because of the challenges they presented. I would wake up every day for weeks on end with urgent text messages from my contractor, asking me for my thoughts on fixtures, outlet placements, trim colors—just an onslaught of minute details that would give anyone decision fatigue. Maybe that's how you're feeling right now about the current phase of your healing journey. The anticipation of a life change may have been exciting and motivating at first, but now you're faced with a myriad of practical decisions you have to make in order to live out this new life:

- How do I leave that toxic relationship?
- How can I save enough money for therapy?

- How many times do I have to struggle with the same emotional triggers?
- Is making all these changes even worth the trouble?

Trust me, I've been there. I get it. Taking ownership of your life is a monumental task . . . but that's exactly how monuments are built—with tiny bricks and teeny tiles, one exhaustive piece at a time. Those small decisions will ultimately give you the forever home of your dreams. I'm relieved I took the time to address all of these small demands now that I get to enjoy my new house. These details are what make the home safer, more comfortable, and more enjoyable to live in. Despite my exhaustion and headaches during different phases of the project, I knew that much of the work only had to be done once. As I move forward, only light maintenance is required to maintain the remarkable structure that was built.

Friend, you have the power to push through the hard parts. If taking ownership feels hard, it means you're on the right path. It's not easy, but it will always, *always* be worth it. Are you ready to take the next step?

Anyone who belongs to Christ has become a new person. The old life is gone; a new life has begun!

2 CORINTHIANS 5:17

Just for You

Friend, feel free to take a deep breath and reflect on all the knowledge you've gained. When you're ready, consider the prompts below.

1. What ongoing thought or emotion are you having a hard time owning?
2. Where did that difficult thought or emotion originate?
3. What one step can you take to start owning your life more fully?

Let's Pray Together

Dear heavenly Father, thank you for allowing me the opportunity to steward my body and my life well. I ask that you give me the courage to take ownership of my body, thoughts, and feelings. As I wrestle to make sense of my difficult emotions, empower me to approach these hurting parts of myself with the same love and compassion you've shown me. Just as you've begun to redeem my painful experiences, I pray that you will also redeem my broken relationship with myself. Thank you for teaching me by example what it means to fully embrace ownership of my life. In Jesus' name. Amen.

Chapter 11

Cultivating Godly Mindfulness

The key is in accepting your thoughts, all of them, even the bad ones. Accept thoughts, but don't become them.

Matt Haig, *Reasons to Stay Alive*

*T*oward the end of our renovation process, I remember cheerfully driving to our new house on a sunny afternoon to check on its progress. I pulled into the driveway, unlocked the front door, and casually strolled into the living room—my favorite place in the house. To my confusion, stretched across the newly laid vinyl floor was a glassy surface of water. "Huh," I said in a daze. Then it hit me. *Why is the entire living room flooded?* The water had already flooded our electric fireplace and floor vents. I followed the trickling sound and found another steady stream flowing into our garage. It was a disaster! I attempted to kick the water out through our back door with exasperated, sweeping kicks, to no avail. I pulled out my phone and dialed our contractor for help.

"Don't worry, I'll try to get someone to come out!" he assured me. In the meantime, I gathered all the rolls of paper towels I could find in the construction area and attempted to soak up the water. I could've thrown maybe a dozen rolls in there and the room still would've been saturated by the flood. Panic-stricken, I grabbed the outdoor broom and tried to sweep the water out—again, to no avail. Heartsick, I knelt and thought of all the potential problems this one issue would cause. Both Jon and I had already maxed out of energy as we worked to balance our jobs with this renovation. If the water were to spread any farther, I didn't know how we would be able to manage reconstructing the damaged space.

Perhaps you're familiar with that sense of panic and overwhelm. Rebuilding your life after trauma can feel a lot like taking two steps forward and three steps back. Despite the enormous time and effort you put into improving your mental health, all it takes is one particular trigger to undo all of your progress. Even seemingly small things, like a misunderstanding or criticism, may send you spiraling into feelings of betrayal, rejection, or abandonment. You may have taken therapy courses, read books, and made changes in your relationships. Yet you're still feeling stuck in certain areas because of emotional trauma, which can feel like it has a choke hold on your life, despite your hard work and efforts to heal. You are not alone in this struggle. It's important to acknowledge the root cause of your fears and address them with self-compassion and patience. Remember that healing is a journey, not a destination, and progress is still progress, no matter how small.

Valid Reasons for Harmful Vices

In his bestseller titled *In the Realm of Hungry Ghosts*, Dr. Gabor Maté explains, "Not all addictions are rooted in abuse or trauma, but I do believe they can all be traced to painful experience. A hurt is at the center of *all* addictive behaviors. It is present in the gambler, the Internet addict, the compulsive shopper, and the workaholic."[1] There are always valid reasons underneath our habits and addictions.

We can respond to our addictions in three different ways. Many people justify their vice by saying it's not as bad as that person's way of coping. After all, it does appear on the surface that being a workaholic might be better than getting inebriated at a bar—especially because the American capitalism culture rewards overworking. However, distracting ourselves with work and numbing ourselves with alcohol both fail to address the root issue. You simply can't put a piece of tape over a leaking pipe and expect it to stop flooding your home.

The second response is continuing to ignore the wound and hoping for the best. However, even minor wounds can produce infection when we let them fester. Just like the leaking pipes in my home renovation, disregarded wounds don't just go away; they cause significant damage over time.

The third response is to wake up to the deeper issues at hand. This is certainly easier said than done. Yet there is a way to regain emotional stability and uproot the things from your past that are holding you back. The answer comes in three steps:

1. Becoming mindful of what our emotions are trying to tell us.
2. Fully accepting our emotions by approaching them with the 8 Cs unveiled later in this chapter (page 190).
3. Leading our emotions lovingly, just as Jesus leads us with unconditional love, kindness, and patience.

Think before You Speak

When I was in fifth grade, I showed up to school in my father's old T-shirts and socks. Classmates would laugh at how the heels of my socks would ride up the back of my Skechers because they were so comically oversized. The teachers at my elementary school knew me as nothing more than a rambunctious tomboy. One teacher even thought of me as a complete troublemaker because of my outspokenness, and another labeled me a "future borderline performer in school" because they didn't think I would be equipped for university, despite my above-average grades. I moved through these formative years feeling heavily misunderstood and quite ashamed of who I was, until I met a teacher who favored me for the first time. Her name was Mrs. Lopez.

Despite my rough appearance (and crude, open-mouthed chewing), my fifth-grade teacher saw something special in my creativity and gave me opportunities other teachers never would. She noticed my outspokenness and volunteered me for school emceeing opportunities. She saw my crafting in class and used it as an example for our final art project. She even invited me to her son's birthday party! I reveled in her compassion and favoritism because even at that age, I had the capacity to realize that she had chosen to love a child whom others deemed unlovable.

During parent-teacher meetings, Mrs. Lopez would always gush about what a gifted student I was and how much integrity I put into each of my projects. "The only thing she needs to learn, though, is how to think before she speaks," Mrs. Lopez warned my mother, who nodded enthusiastically. My mother then glanced at me for a Vietnamese translation, but I'd just smile and mistranslate it into something else. Mrs. Lopez then handed over my report card, which showed neat rows of A's lined next to each subject, ending with a "Notes" section that would never fail to say, "Remember to think before you speak!"

Years later, I still remember the repeated feedback from the teacher who genuinely loved me and wanted the best for my future. *Think before you speak*, I'd tell myself before any important event, and it would prove to be a crucial reminder to have more self-awareness, lest I embarrass myself or unknowingly hurt someone with my words. The older I got, the easier it became to pause and do an internal inspection of my emotions before I spoke.

However, all this mindfulness generally goes out the door the second I become emotionally triggered. Perhaps you know what I mean. On a normal, happy day, you wouldn't categorize yourself as a rageful, depressed, or bitter person. Yet all it takes is for one car to cut you off on the freeway for you to become enraged and carry that anger with you back home. Or a loved one may inappropriately comment on your weight, which leads you to become depressed and feel guilty about eating all week. It often only takes one trigger to prompt the unhealthy response you've tried so hard to keep at bay. To gain mastery over our emotional reactions, the key is to cultivate mindfulness. By being proactive and centered, we can prepare for the trigger before it strikes and reclaim control over our responses.

What Is Mindfulness?

As Christians, practicing mindfulness means intentionally aligning our hearts with the heart of the Father and approaching our inner emotions with calmness, compassion, and curiosity. Mindfulness is the first step not only toward self-control but also toward achieving the peace and harmony we seek in our lives. By reflecting the unconditional love of the Father through mindful living, we can break free from the cycle of neglecting our inner selves and truly attend to the parts of us that have been misheard, misattuned, and misunderstood. Mindfulness is about giving ourselves permission to heal and grow.

The Bible affirms the importance of mindfulness by emphasizing the fruit of the Spirit (see Galatians 5:22–23), such as love, joy, peace, patience, kindness, goodness, faithfulness, gentleness, and self-control. By cultivating a mindful heart that is attuned to God and others, we can manifest these qualities in our daily lives.

Throughout the Bible, we find numerous examples of the value of godly mindfulness:

1. "God gave us a spirit not of fear but of power and love and self-control" (2 Timothy 1:7 ESV).

Mindfulness

is about giving

ourselves permission to

heal and grow.

2. "Guard your heart above all else, for it determines the course of your life" (Proverbs 4:23).
3. "Don't worry about anything; instead, pray about everything. Tell God what you need, and thank him for all he has done" (Philippians 4:6).
4. "Don't copy the behavior and customs of this world, but let God transform you into a new person by changing the way you think. Then you will learn to know God's will for you, which is good and pleasing and perfect" (Romans 12:2).
5. The entirety of Psalm 23—and many more.

Three Ways to Practice Godly Mindfulness

We have a great variety of ways to practice mindfulness that align with the Scriptures and honor God. I will list the three techniques that work best for me:

1. **Breathe.** Breathing exercises can slow down the heart rate, help us feel more centered, and ultimately create space to bring our anxious thoughts to the Lord. One of my favorite breathing exercises is called box breathing. Slowly inhale through your nose for four counts, hold your breath for four counts,

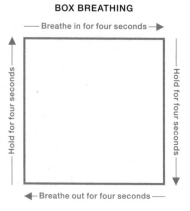

    BOX BREATHING

    ── Breathe in for four seconds ──▶

    Hold for four seconds

    Hold for four seconds

    ◀── Breathe out for four seconds ──

    and slowly exhale through your mouth for four counts. You can repeat this technique as many times as necessary to feel more relaxed.

2. **Integrate.** Integrate reflective activities into your daily routine so that mindfulness can become second nature to you. My three nonnegotiable checkpoints throughout the day are writing in my devotional journal in the morning, walking my corgi in the afternoon, and praying in the evening. No matter how busy my days get, I've resolved to always protect these three nonnegotiables. I realize I'm a more loving and Christlike person when I make time for these mindful activities. If you love an enriching routine, try integrating two or three nonnegotiable mindful activities throughout your day—sacred times when you can retreat into a solitary place and commune with the Lord. Remember that quality time with God was a nonnegotiable that kept Jesus resilient, resolute, and faithful to the end (Luke 5:15–16).

3. **Disrupt.** If you are not used to daily reflections and need more accountability, you can disrupt your normal schedule by setting alarms throughout the day to check in with yourself. My husband was advised by his counselor to do this because he often got lost in the routine of his work. Before

he'd know it, the whole day would fly by before he even had a chance to take time for himself. By the time he got done with work, he would be exhausted and have nothing left to give to anyone. Per his counselor's advice, he started setting an alarm right after his first meeting, another one after lunch, and a third one after work. Each time the alarm rang, he'd ask himself these three questions:

- What am I thinking?
- What am I feeling?
- What am I doing?

By doing these mental, emotional, and physical scans, Jon was finally able to meet his own needs throughout the day and self-regulate. If he's feeling bothered by the events of his day, he can now label his emotions, check where he feels the most anxiety in his body, and then go for a relaxing walk or take a coffee break. These self-check-ins have vastly improved his body aches, overall mood, and capacity to be present with his friends and family throughout the week.

No Bad Parts

The first time I became genuinely mindful of my own heart was when I discovered internal family systems (IFS)—a form of trauma therapy that approaches the mind as a system of parts rather than as one unified whole. By directing our attention toward the parts of ourselves that have been ignored or cast aside, we can begin to cultivate true mindfulness. IFS is a powerful tool for helping us uncover and connect with these neglected parts, leading to deeper healing and self-awareness.

The movie *Inside Out* can be viewed as a quirky yet insightful example of internal family systems. Just like the characters Joy, Fear, Anger, Disgust, and Sadness in the movie, our internal family members can have alliances, hostility, estrangement, and discord. But at the end of the day, they all have the common goal of protecting us. With the help of IFS, we can get to know these characters and work toward a harmonious family dynamic within ourselves.

IFS was an unexpected addition on my therapy journey. I reached out to my therapist Cathy with anxiety about revisiting a memory during EMDR, and she introduced me to IFS as an alternative. It was a game-changing moment.

At Cathy's recommendation, I read a book called *No Bad Parts* by Dr. Richard Schwartz, the founder of IFS. Dr. Schwartz was originally a family therapist, but he soon realized that each family member had their own inner family too. With his groundbreaking discovery, he helped his clients understand and heal their internal family systems, leading to life-changing breakthroughs.

IFS assumes that the mind is a system of parts with unique personalities, fears, and desires, as seen in the characters of *Inside Out*. While these parts can create chaos when burdened, they can also serve valuable roles when functioning at their best. For example, Anger helps establish boundaries, Fear promotes safety, Disgust provides individuality, and Joy and Sadness work together to foster empathy.

It turned out that my fear of EMDR stemmed from my Manager part, a perfectionist who dresses like an executive secretary and always seeks to uphold my reputation. Though helpful at times, she can also be overly critical and demanding. Even when other parts of me are quiet, my inner Manager is always present, ready to assist me in my endeavors.

It may sound like science fiction, but this type of internal exploration can lead to remarkable breakthroughs for people who need help working through their trauma. IFS treats our minds like a symphony, with each part playing its own unique melody. By approaching our minds in this compassionate way, we can learn to understand and work with even the most challenging parts of ourselves. This approach can help us gently bring to light our past hurts, and especially bring them to Jesus, who can help us unburden and heal. And just as we model Jesus' compassion and grace toward the outcasts of society, we can release our internal parts from the negative emotions that they may carry from past experiences. Even seemingly negative parts like my inner Manager can turn into powerful allies for personal growth and transformation when they are unburdened.

The Christlike Response

In IFS, there is a concept of the self that is separate from its burdened parts, which Dr. Schwartz describes as a calm, confident, compassionate, and curious leader of its internal family system. There is a true self hidden inside each of us, no matter how broken or traumatized we may be. This is the one character that is missing from *Inside Out*—a wise inner parent who could guide the family of parts whenever they felt out of control.

To unburden the wounded parts of ourselves, we first must activate our inner self, but this can be challenging for those who have experienced trauma and are used to being in fight-or-flight mode. The protective parts of our inner family are quick to respond and often resort to fixing, numbing, or destroying perceived threats. However, by practicing mindfulness and asking ourselves if we are feeling anxious, avoidant, or despairing, we can identify and connect with these activated parts. We can then reassure them that we care about, honor, and protect them, validating their fears and empathizing with their struggles. Over time, our inner parts will learn to trust our leadership, paving the way for healing and growth.

The best way to learn how to do this is to consult with a trauma-informed therapist who has experience with IFS. While it can be empowering to engage in self-discovery and attempt to communicate with our inner exiles and protectors, it's important to note that the process can sometimes be overwhelming, especially when protective parts are hesitant to allow communication with exiled parts. With the help of a trained therapist, however, we can navigate these internal conversations in a safe and productive way.

As we engage in IFS therapy and cultivate a stronger sense of self, we can extend to our burdened parts the same love and wisdom that Christ embodies. The state of accessing your true self is characterized by these eight Cs:[2]

1. Curiosity
2. Calm
3. Confidence
4. Compassion
5. Creativity
6. Clarity
7. Courage
8. Connectedness

Jesus is the ultimate example of someone who is always in self mode regardless of his circumstances. There were moments when Jesus was angered, but in his anger he did not sin. We also see instances when Jesus was deeply anguished. The Scriptures state that his sweat was like drops of blood in Gethsemane right before his crucifixion (see Luke 22:44). Still, in his distress, he surrendered his will to God the Father. Jesus demonstrated that being in self mode does not mean you cannot be afflicted; it means you can still have faith and self-regulate in the face of extreme distress.

This gives new meaning to the apostle Paul's words: "I no longer live, but Christ lives in me" (Galatians 2:20 NIV). When we give our lives to Jesus, we gain the Holy Spirit, who gives us the power and ability to be Christlike even in the most triggering situations. All of this takes practice, patience, and a continuous influx of love to sustain. Knowing that we are loved by God gives us the fuel to love our inner exiles as well as the external outcasts of society.

Though himself not a Christian, Dr. Schwartz shared, "What I found is that love is the answer in the inner world, just as it is in the outer world. . . . Through a Christian lens, through IFS people wind up doing in the inner world what Jesus did in the outer—they go to inner exiles and enemies with love, heal them, and bring them home, just as he did with the lepers, the poor, and the outcasts."[3] What a beautiful depiction of God's unconditional love! As you confront your deepest fears and anxieties with empathy, you will guide your inner exiles toward healing and growth in a profound expression of Christlike love.

I encourage you to take a moment to look inward and consider which parts may have been shamed by others, burdened by trauma, and maybe even exiled by you. Perhaps you, like me, have a strong manager part that takes over when you face uncertainty or instability. Maybe you have a firefighter part that tries to put out the fires of your overwhelming emotions by numbing you with addictions and substances. Or maybe you have a young inner child who needs you to witness their experience. Or you may have all three, and many other parts as well. The second you give credence to the existence of your inner family system, you allow yourself to experience a state of mindfulness you never thought possible.

I pray that as you embark on this next chapter, the Lord

will unveil your eyes to the parts of you that most need love, gentleness, and compassion. May you follow in Jesus' footsteps by approaching your inner exiles with love and bringing them home, just as he did with the outcasts. In Jesus' name. Amen.

You are not controlled by your sinful nature. You are controlled by the Spirit if you have the Spirit of God living in you.

ROMANS 8:9

Just for You

This is your time to pause and consider all the new information you've just absorbed. When you're ready, feel free to reflect on the prompts below.

1. Let's do a quick body scan. Are you currently in an activated state or a calm state? Describe your physical senses in detail.
2. Do you find it challenging to extend the eight Cs toward yourself at this moment (curiosity, calm, confidence, and so forth)?
3. How does learning about IFS change the way you want to approach your internal family members (if applicable)?

Dear heavenly Father, thank you for demonstrating your unconditional love for me through Jesus. I pray that you will help me develop a deeper awareness of my body, thoughts, and emotions. I pray for the strength and courage to face my inner struggles with compassion, curiosity, and connection. Guide me toward loving and accepting all parts of myself, especially the wounded and hurting parts. Just as you have shown me mercy and grace, I want to learn how to extend that same grace to my inner children. Thank you for showing me that the pathway to healing can be sweet when you are traveling beside me. In Jesus' name. Amen.

Chapter 12
Forgiving the Unforgivable

Your greatest test will be how you handle people who mishandled you.

Unknown

*W*hen I was in fourth grade, I saw a kid aggressively pull down my classmate Kelly* from the monkey bars. Kelly fell hard into the ditch below and cried out in pain before getting up to confront her perpetrator. By the time a teacher arrived at the scene, both children seemed equally flustered. In hindsight, the teacher probably thought that both children were exaggerating and wanted to put a quick stop to the quarrel before it got out of control.

Despite the fact that many witnesses told the teacher that Kelly was the one pulled down from the monkey bars, the teacher made both children apologize to each other and call it good. Not a word of care and concern was uttered to Kelly, whose arms and legs were starting to bruise from the fall. It seemed to me at the time that the teacher didn't want to be inconvenienced by the incident. Once the teacher was gone, the perpetrator teased a hurt and disheartened Kelly with a mocking "Ha-ha!"

From that moment on, Kelly shut down in class and never behaved like her lively self in front of our teachers again. How could she? She had been physically bullied by a student and was met with a callous demand to forgive before she received any compassion, time, or reason to forgive. Kelly could no longer trust our teachers the same way after her experience of betrayal.

You may have experienced that kind of injustice—the kind where it was clear that you were wronged and yet the people you turned to for help treated you like an inconvenience. Rather than

---

* "Kelly" (pseud.).

receiving comfort, validation, and protection from them, you received blame, apathy, and a callous suggestion to "just forgive." This type of reaction can be profoundly hurtful when it happens in the church, and even more so if it happens in your own family.

You may have had people weaponize Bible verses to shame you into forgiving. "If you don't forgive others, then God won't forgive you," they say—without recognizing their own unwillingness to empathize with you or sit with you in your pain. They forget equally important biblical principles such as, "Carry each other's burdens, and in this way you will fulfill the law of Christ" (Galatians 6:2 NIV). To carry each other's burdens is to share in their pain without trying to dismiss or fix it. Being present with someone who is hurting requires us to demonstrate empathy, and empathy is the most powerful way to forgive the unforgivable.

Rather than forcing ourselves to forgive our enemies, a more effective approach is to first fill our tanks with love, affection,

Empathy can put out anger like water extinguishes a flame, so *forgiveness* will be the natural outcome.

and empathy. Empathy can put out anger like water extinguishes a flame, so forgiveness will be the natural outcome. If the teacher had taken the time to empathize with Kelly's pain and humiliation, perhaps Kelly would have been more likely to forgive her bully in her heart. Instead of receiving empathy, however, Kelly received apathy. Her emotional tank was not filled by anyone, so she had nothing left to give.

Empathy is what God showed us when he sent his only Son to be born in a lowly manger. Despite our brokenness and rebellion toward him, God had empathy for the human condition. Out of his empathetic love, he sent Jesus to bear the punishment for our sin so that our relationship with him could be restored. He gave us the capacity to forgive the unforgivable in others when he forgave the unforgivable in us. When we recall just how much we have been forgiven, loved, and restored by God, our natural response to those who have wronged us is to forgive them as well. This chapter is designed to help you fully grasp the depth of God's overflowing grace and forgiveness. Through him, your emotional tank can be filled to the brim with compassion, forgiveness, and empathy.

Who to Forgive

Asking ourselves who we need to forgive is a crucial first step toward healing, but the answer can be quite complex and nuanced. As demonstrated by Kelly's experience, she was hurt not only by her bully but also by her teacher's lack of intervention. It's essential to take the time to thoroughly examine the situation and identify all the parties involved in causing us pain. Failure to do so can lead to a general mistrust of others who may resemble the original perpetrators, triggering our survival instincts and hindering our ability to respond appropriately.

By taking the time to name those who hurt us, we ground

ourselves in reality and gain the clarity needed to move toward forgiveness and healing. So if you've been hurt by multiple parties, be sure to inspect your heart and identify the specific people who caused your pain. Through this self-reflection, you can respond with wisdom and proportionality to the situation at hand, paving the way toward emotional restoration.

If our reactions are disproportionate to the situation, it may indicate that we are subconsciously reliving a past trauma. For instance, Jon and I once had a weekend full of tension when we couldn't see eye to eye on anything and ended up having a heated argument on Sunday evening. As we tried to understand why we were feeling so tense, we discovered that both of us had received messages on Friday from our family members that triggered our anxiety. These separate conflicts with our family members touched on deep emotional wounds, which led us to treat each other roughly that weekend.

Once we became aware of this, we were able to apologize to each other and make amends. By taking a moment to reflect on our emotions and past experiences, we identified who we truly needed to forgive—our family members. This introspection allowed us to approach the situation with more clarity and compassion. Sometimes the person who is triggering your hurt may not be the one who created your wound. When we investigate the true source of our emotions, we can keep ourselves from bleeding on the ones who did not cut us.

What to Forgive

The next step toward forgiveness is a powerful one: identifying exactly what needs to be forgiven. This mindful pause allows us to assess the situation and bear witness to our own pain. It's an opportunity to take control of our emotions and find clarity. Journaling can be a valuable tool in this process, helping us articulate our thoughts and emotions with greater depth and insight. By taking the time to reflect and understand the impact of the situation, we can move forward with a greater sense of empowerment and self-awareness.

A close friend once shared how she had been verbally and physically abused by her older brother throughout her life. With tears in her eyes, she said, "I wasn't even able to call it abuse until maybe five years ago. I just wanted to protect my brother so much that I lied to myself." Bearing witness to her own abuse was crucial to receiving the breakthrough she desperately needed. Acknowledging that the people whom we trusted and relied on for protection have caused us harm is an incredibly difficult task. Our inner protectors often make excuses for those who hurt us, shielding us from feelings of vulnerability. To avoid the intense pain and humiliation of our wounded inner child, we build walls of defense, leaving our wounded parts neglected and exiled within our internal family system. However, by recognizing and facing the truth of the harm done, we can begin to break down those walls and bring healing to those neglected parts of ourselves.

When I asked my friend how she was able to reach that inner breakthrough, she said, "One day, I felt God nudging me to be specific about what I needed to forgive. That was when I went through my list of offenses one by one and called out the abuse for what it was. I needed to admit to myself that it should not have happened, and then I was fully able to forgive." She shared that it took almost thirty years to finally come to this realization, but I assured her that this accomplishment was no easy feat. Some people never reach this point of emotional breakthrough.

What my friend demonstrated was nothing short of Christlike empathy for her inner child. At the Holy Spirit's nudging, she courageously approached her inner exile—the one who had been locked away for more than thirty years—and bore witness to her pain. She no longer made excuses for her abuser. Instead, she listened, validated, and liberated her inner child from her pain and bitterness. It was the type of forgiveness that can only be achieved through Christlike empathy.

Did you know that among the seven things that God detests the most is a false witness (see Proverbs 6:16–19)? Yet many of us have been so brainwashed into invalidating our own experiences that we become false witnesses for ourselves. I encourage you to be a reliable witness to your own pain. Spend time in solitude with the Lord and ask him to help you detail exactly what it was that happened to you. Ask the Holy Spirit to help you resist the urge to make excuses for your perpetrators or blame yourself for what happened. Vindicate your inner child by being specific with all the ways you were harmed. Then and only then can you truly start to forgive.

How to Forgive

The concept of forgiveness is often lauded as a noble and virtuous ideal, but in practice, forgiveness can be incredibly challenging to embody. Despite the countless resources available on the topic, many of us still grapple with how to apply forgiveness in our lives. Perhaps this is because we as human beings are wired to seek justice and fairness. When we are wronged, our innate sense of justice cries out for retribution or restitution, leaving little room for forgiveness. It is not enough to simply will ourselves into forgiving someone, since our natural desire for justice is too strong to ignore.

Yet unforgiveness is like a slow rot in the framing of our house. It's easy to convince ourselves that we can push aside feelings of resentment and anger, but in reality, they are insidious and can weaken the very structure of our lives. Just like a stubborn mold that persistently grows, unforgiveness can twist and distort our sense of trust, leaving us feeling isolated and alone.

Time and justice are two crucial elements when it comes to forgiveness. While it may sound ideal to immediately forgive someone who has wronged us, our emotions need time to process and heal from the trauma. Just as a physical wound needs time to heal, our emotional wounds also require time to mend. It's okay to feel hurt, angry, or sad about what has happened to us. These emotions are a natural response to trauma, and they deserve to be acknowledged and validated. Rushing the process may result in our pain being suppressed rather than properly addressed.

Forgiveness requires us to confront our deepest hurts head-on. It's not just a matter of saying, "I forgive you," and moving on. For true forgiveness to occur, justice must be served

By surrendering our hurt and anger to *God* and allowing his *grace* to transform us from the inside out, we can find true *peace.*

in some way. When we experience a wrong, we have a natural desire for justice to be served. However, it is important to recognize that justice doesn't always come in the form of revenge or punishment; sometimes it can come from simply acknowledging the wrong that was done and taking steps to prevent it from happening again. As Christians, we have access to a powerful tool for forgiveness—the grace of God. By surrendering our hurt and anger to God and allowing his grace to transform us from the inside out, we can find true peace and resolution in our hearts. This process takes time and effort, but the rewards are immeasurable.

I once experienced betrayal from one of my closest friends. She was someone I trusted with all of my secrets and resources, and I treated her like family. I never thought she would purposely hurt me, but during her journey of self-discovery, she did something that made me feel deeply wronged.

At first, I was hurt and angry. I couldn't believe I had shared so much of myself with someone who could be so careless with our friendship. I anguished over the betrayal for days, feeling lost and unsure of how to console the part of me that felt so hurt.

It was during this difficult time that I turned to my Bible and opened to the book of Psalms. As I began to read David's heart-wrenching cries, I felt a sense of comfort and relief wash over me. Right on the first page of Psalm 1, I found a comparison between the righteous (those who delight in the law of the Lord) and the wicked (those who delight in the ruin of others): "Sinners will have no place among the godly. For the LORD watches over the path of the godly, but the path of the wicked leads to destruction" (Psalm 1:5–6). This passage reassured me that God cares about justice and that his favor and protection are upon me. I did not have to worry about seeking my own justice because he was watching over me and had seen all that transpired behind my back. This was indeed a reassuring passage.

As I continued reading Psalm 2, I was struck by the parallels between the feeling of betrayal I had experienced and the betrayal that God endured at the hands of his people. The psalm described how the kings and rulers of the earth plotted together against the Lord and his anointed one, saying, "Let us break their chains and throw off their shackles" (Psalm 2:3 NIV). I couldn't believe what I was reading. It was as if God was directly empathizing with me by showing how he also was betrayed by his people. His pain must have run even deeper than mine because these were the people he had created in his own image. It reminded me that I was not alone in my pain and that even the almighty Creator had felt the sting of betrayal. If anyone could feel the depths of my anguish, it was God himself.

Psalm 2 also revealed God's promises to his chosen king: "The LORD said to me, 'You are my son. Today I have become your Father. Only ask, and I will give you the nations as your inheritance, the whole earth as your possession'" (Psalm 2:7–8). It was like a beautiful affirmation of my worth and value in his eyes. The Lord was speaking to David, and I felt like he was also declaring these words over me:

> You are my daughter. Today I have become your Father. Ask for what you need and I will not forsake you. I won't withhold good things from you. Everything that I have is also yours.

That much was true. As the apostle Paul wrote, we are "heirs of God and co-heirs with Christ" (Romans 8:17 NIV). As I read through these promises, I felt like God was speaking directly to my inner child who had been deeply hurt by this betrayal. He spoke to her using the words from Psalm 2 to affirm her precious identity in him and remind her that he has her covered.

The Scriptures brought me to tears. While my anger had already been assuaged by this point, I was still unsure how I could possibly forgive my friend for mishandling our friendship. But I felt the Holy Spirit nudging me to turn to Psalm 3, where I found even more powerful words of comfort and healing.

Now this was exactly the kind of psalm I had hoped to read when I flipped open my Bible. This psalm was filled with verses like, "Strike all my enemies on the jaw," and "Break the teeth of the wicked" (Psalm 3:7 NIV)—all very satisfying stuff for someone who felt bitter and betrayed. But at this point, I didn't need it anymore. I already felt vindicated enough because of the first two psalms, and I questioned why I was convicted to read this third psalm. I turned to the sidebar in the margin for clarity, and my eyes lit up at the title: "Finding Justice in the Midst of Injustice." This was precisely why I turned to God for help—to seek justice. I read on:

> While most readers probably cannot relate to the exact circumstances described, they can recall events in their own lives when people have wounded them deeply. They can identify with David's request for divine justice. . . . Psalms like this remind readers that God does not turn a blind eye to injustice and sweep it under the cosmic carpet. Instead, he chose to unleash his wrath against sin on his own Son and, in so doing, make right all wrongs, pay all debts and free all captives.[1]

What a resolve! I had never felt so relieved of bitterness in my life. I had encountered God's convictions before, but this experience was different. Through his Word, he showed me that he was intimately acquainted with my pain and willing to sit with me in it. His love and patience with me in the midst of my struggle moved me to tears. To feel acknowledged and heard by God in such a profound way was a powerful moment of divine connection.

Out of his great mercy, God nudged me to explore more deeply the reasons why forgiveness was not only possible but necessary. I had been holding on to my bitterness, unable to let go of the hurt and betrayal I had experienced. But God didn't condemn me for my struggle. Instead, he met me where I was and gently guided me toward a deeper understanding of his grace. He showed me that forgiveness wasn't just about "getting over it" or "letting it go"—it was about something much more profound. Through his Word, I was assured that he would never give a free pass to injustice. As the almighty Judge, he would not have it in his character to "sweep injustice under the cosmic carpet."

Sin must always be punished, so I didn't need to worry about convincing God to care about my injustice. He cared so deeply that he had already made sure to exact punishment for that sin through the sacrifice of Jesus Christ. Because Jesus had already borne the sins that my friend committed against me, I could truly feel released from all of my grudges and bitterness. He already paid her debt in full. Because of Jesus' sacrifice, I was free to forgive, free to let go of my anger and resentment, and free to move forward in the abundant life he had planned for me.

When we are in Christ, we not only have the *power* to forgive but also a satisfying *reason* to forgive. If you are struggling to forgive someone in your life right now, know that God does not shame you for feeling hurt and angry. Bring your most honest, heart-wrenching cries to him. He does not condemn you for your yearning for divine justice. He empathizes with you because he has been there many times through many millennia. He can handle the depths of your sorrow and will never abandon you in your suffering. Like the psalmist David, you can complain to God all you want with your most heartfelt cries of lament. He will accept it all and still affirm his love and adoration for you.

Once you are released from your immediate pain, let him remind you of why he sent his Son to be crucified. God takes our burdens so seriously that he was willing to bear it all on our behalf, so that we can be fully restored to wholeness when we put our faith in Jesus. Think of the most horrendous betrayal you have ever experienced—Jesus willingly bore *that* on the cross for both you *and* the person who hurt you. Unbearable betrayal can only be resolved by uncompromising justice, and such justice can only be redeemed by unconditional love. This is the perfect picture of who God is—fully just and fully gracious.

I pray that as you cry out to him in the midst of your injustice, you will experience a reawakening of the gospel in your soul. There may be one person you could not find the will to forgive, no matter how many years have passed, but I pray that you will finally experience tangible relief as God empathizes with your pain and removes your burdens. May his words of comfort and counsel lead you back to where it all began—with his Son, Jesus. In his name I pray. Amen.

> **Now, most people would not be willing to die for an upright person, though someone might perhaps be willing to die for a person who is especially good. But God showed his great love for us by sending Christ to die for us while we were still sinners.**
>
> **ROMANS 5:7-8**

Just for You

Now is the time to take a moment and process all the knowledge you've gained. When you're ready, explore the reflection prompts below.

1. Did you have any preconceived notions or misconceptions about forgiveness?
2. Have you experienced any hurts or offenses that you find difficult to forgive?
3. How does your faith in Jesus impact your ability to forgive those who have wronged you?

Let's Pray Together

Dear heavenly Father, thank you for the gift of forgiveness through your Son, Jesus. I pray that you will help me understand the depth of your forgiveness and show me how to extend this same forgiveness to others. Empower me to let go of my resentment and bitterness and to accept that you have already paid the debt for those who have hurt me. Thank you for giving me not only the power to forgive others but also a satisfying reason to forgive them. May I continue to grow in my understanding of the depths of your sacrifice on our behalf. In Jesus' name. Amen.

Adorn

Section 4

*What joy for those you choose
to bring near,
those who live in your holy
courts.
What festivities await us
inside your holy Temple.*

Psalm 65:4

209

*T*his is it. You've stood amid the rubble of your old life and trusted the Lord to lay your new foundation. You've then erected a solid framework of boundaries and inspected the inner workings of your new life to make sure you've left nothing unaddressed. Now you finally get to be settled into this new, extraordinary life you've built with God's blessing and guidance—a life that feels more like home than you had ever thought possible.

The adornment phase may sound like the most fun part of a home renovation, but it also requires intentionality and introspection. What are the elements that make you uniquely you? What kind of energy do you need to thrive? Would you like your home to inspire a sense of calm or motivate you? These are all questions to consider during the adornment phase of your renovation. Adornment is just as much about practicality as it is about beauty. It is the careful curation of light fixtures, fabrics, and furniture that makes a home feel lived in and loved. What you choose to adorn your life with will show in the way you carry yourself in the world.

This is your chance to adorn your newly built life with the beautiful gifts God has in store for you—gifts such as love, peace, beauty, joy, and wisdom. After all, you've waited quite a while to get to a point where you can adorn your new life with elements that bring you joy. The thought of having a fulfilling life adorned with these abundant gifts may take some time to get used to, but I promise that these gifts are meant for *you*.

As you journey through this final section, you will be invited to partake in creative calls to action that will help you experience the tangible abundance that God desires for you. Although you may feel like some of these abundant blessings are too good to be true, I pray that your inner critics will be graciously won over when they taste how generous and trustworthy God really is. May you find the courage to let God adorn your life with the gifts he has long prepared for you.

Chapter 13
Learning to Receive

Jesus answered her, "If you knew the gift of God and who it is that asks you for a drink, you would have asked him, and he would have given you living water."

John 4:10 NIV

After months of waiting, problem solving, and endless redesigns, I had finally stepped into my forever home. The silence that greeted me was oh so satisfying—a stark contrast from the noisy months of renovations that had gone before. I had poured my heart and soul into designing and reconstructing this space, taking on every problem and setback with determination and resilience. And now as I stood in the midst of the finished product, I felt like I was walking in a dream. Every detail, from floor tiles to wall paint, had been carefully chosen and crafted to create the perfect space. *Surreal* is an understatement.

In an instant, my mind became focused, my shoulders became unclenched, and my heartbeat slowed to a tranquil rhythm. As I gazed around the room, I was captivated by the warm glow of natural light streaming through our bifold doors, illuminating the entire family room. The waterfall kitchen island shimmered like a jewel. I lifted my eyes to count the ceiling beams, and it felt as though they stretched on infinitely. The air was fresh and crisp, the space vast and open, and every corner exuded a dazzling radiance that left me awestruck. As Jon and I continued to explore our new home, marveling at its beauty and spaciousness, a nagging sense of guilt began to creep up on me.

The internal family system within me felt unworthy of this beautiful new home. It had everything we could have hoped for, but its abundance left me feeling uneasy and suspicious. I was not used to receiving blessings without conditions. Isn't it ironic how we can become so accustomed to our suffering that we reject God's answers to our prayers? Our past trauma conditions us to view stability as untrustworthy, and everything inside us tells us to stay on high alert for the next crisis to hit. While searching for the next bad thing to happen, we miss out on the good we currently have. That is the double-edged sword of having a heightened internal alarm system—you seem more prepared for potential dangers but at the cost of enjoying the safety that already exists.

I caught myself feeling guilty and took a moment to surrender my guilt to the Lord. I prayed, *God, I'm doing the thing where I'm feeling guilty for having peace and stability again. I feel like I'm anticipating the next bad thing to happen because this is too good to be true. Can you please reassure me that this house is a gift from you—that I'm meant to enjoy it?*

I struggled with this tension of excitement for the new home and paranoia that it would all be taken away until that evening, when we strapped our corgi into his harness for a walk around the neighborhood. As we went a few steps out the door, we saw our neighbor across the street running toward us to say hello. He was a kindhearted and jolly man in his mid-fifties who couldn't wait to greet us as neighbors. From our conversation, I learned that he had watched over our home during the renovation process. He made sure no suspicious characters lurked around when no one was there. He officially welcomed us to the neighborhood with the warmest words of encouragement: "Well, it's been a long journey, but the home looks absolutely beautiful. Just take it one day at a time and enjoy what you've built!" I suddenly remembered my prayer to the Lord: *Please reassure me that this house is a gift from you—that I'm meant to enjoy it.* Through the kind words of a friendly next-door neighbor, God affirmed my longing for a forever home and gave me his gracious blessing. In that moment, I felt an undeniable sense of God's divine protection surrounding us, dispelling any fear and guilt lurking in my heart.

If you find yourself in a moment when what you're experiencing seems too good to be true, remember that it is not in God's nature to dampen his blessings with sorrow. In the book of Proverbs, we read, "The blessing of the LORD makes a person rich, and he adds no sorrow with it" (Proverbs 10:22). God's blessings are genuine gifts, free from any conditions or hidden motives. He is a loving Father who desires to bless you with good things. And when you take good care of these blessings, he will entrust you with even more. This is the perfect opportunity to take the reins and step into your new life, adorned with beauty, peace, joy, hope, and wisdom.

How to Receive Graciously

It may sound silly to say this, but as a Vietnamese American woman, I take pride in footing the bill for my friends, even when they protest and insist on paying it. This trait recently surfaced during a brunch with a close friend, who caught me in the act of sneaking away to cover the bill. We must have looked ridiculous to the other diners! However, I know that many Asian American women can relate to this impulse to take care of others—a tendency that often stems from watching our parents selflessly give to others while neglecting their own needs. While giving is a noble trait, it's important to remember that receiving graciously is just as valuable.

My friend emerged as the winner of our "bill tug-of-war" that afternoon, which left me feeling a bit disappointed. But when she noticed my discomfort as she graciously paid for our meal, she offered a pearl of wisdom: "Did you know that you can give at a higher level when you learn to receive?" Her words hit me like a ton of bricks. "I used to struggle with receiving from others too," she went on, "but I realized that if I didn't know how to receive from people, I must be receiving poorly from God as well."

My friend's vulnerability and honesty moved me deeply. Our argument over the check opened up a profound conversation about what it means to be an Asian American woman and a Christian who can accept gifts with grace. If you find yourself giving without being able to receive joyfully, then you are robbed of the reciprocity that God has designed for healthy relationships.

Hyper-independence may seem attractive, but it can actually be detrimental to your overall well-being. It is a heart posture that says, "I cannot rely on anyone to meet my needs." This attitude is often linked to codependency, a pattern in which individuals become excessively reliant on others for validation and fulfillment.

I've witnessed this struggle firsthand in the lives of the strong, capable women in my family. They often vacillate between extreme self-sufficiency and an unspoken longing for someone to take care of them. Unfortunately, when they do voice their needs, their vulnerability is often met with rejection and frustration from those around them. This rejection reinforces their belief that they can only rely on themselves, which leads them back to a state of hyper-independence.

The truth is, we all need connection with and support from others. No one can navigate life entirely on their own. When we reject help and support, we deny ourselves the opportunity to experience the reciprocity and depth of relationships that God designed. By recognizing our own limitations and opening ourselves up to receiving care from others, we can cultivate a deeper sense of humility and grace, which in turn allows us to give and receive love more fully.

Don't let fear of abandonment rob you of the blessings that God has in store for you. You are capable of experiencing long-lasting goodness and stability, even if these things feel unfamiliar to your inner child. You have a new life and a new opportunity to embrace the blessings fully. With God as your foundation and a supportive network to lean on, you can fortify your internal stability and weather any storm that comes your way.

Remember, external stability is never guaranteed, but your internal stability can be strengthened with every passing day. It's time to open your heart and receive the abundance that God wants to pour out on you. Love, peace, beauty, joy, and wisdom are just some of the gifts waiting for you to claim. These amazing and irreplaceable gifts are yours to keep.

Think of these gifts as the exquisite embellishments on the beautiful home you've been renovating. Your hard work has laid a solid foundation, and now it's time to adorn it with the finishing touches that make it truly shine. Embrace this new chapter of your life with open arms, and let God's blessings transform you from the inside out.

Design Your Cozy Nook

I invite you to design a cozy nook in your home that makes you feel safe, happy, and loved. It doesn't have to be big or extravagant, just a beautiful, quiet space reserved for you. You can use it to spend time with the Lord in solitude or to simply take a breather throughout your day. When you walk by this space, let its beauty remind you to rest and relax. This is your opportunity to let yourself experience the tangible feeling of safety you crave.

Here are a few examples of the cozy nooks inside my own home.

My Place of Hope: The Reading Nook and Altar

My reading nook is more than just a cozy corner; it's my personal sanctuary and altar to the Lord. I crafted a minimalist cross artwork using nothing but a canvas, cross, bedsheet, and plaster, which I was excited to share on my Instagram page

(@girlandtheword). This sacred space not only is cherished by my inner child but also serves as a daily reminder of God's unwavering love and grace.

I find peace and comfort every time I pass by my altar or grab a book from my mini library. It's a constant reminder of how far I've come and of how God has faithfully guided me through every obstacle. Jesus used his altar to save me, and

now I'm blessed with the opportunity to create my own altar to honor him. This sacred space is my place of hope, a tangible representation of God's redemptive power in my life. It's a place to which I can always turn for strength and encouragement, no matter what life may throw my way.

My Place of Peace: The Tea Corner

Indulging in the simple pleasure of making tea can be a powerful tool for promoting mindfulness. Each step of the process requires my full attention, allowing me to be completely present in the moment. Whether it's starting my day with a refreshing iced matcha or winding down at night with a soothing cup of chamomile, the act of making tea brings a sense of peace and comfort to my daily routine. Creating a dedicated tea station in your home is a beautiful way to cultivate a space of tranquility. By savoring the experience of tea making, you can foster a deeper connection with yourself and the world around you. Start your day or end your night on a peaceful note with the simple pleasure of an iced or a warm cup of tea.

My Place of Joy: The Houseplant Garden

Gardening is a source of great joy and comfort, as it brings to mind the wonderful memories of my late father, who was a true master of the craft. Despite the challenging living conditions we faced when I was younger, my father always found a way to make our home feel more vibrant and alive by creating beautiful gardens wherever we lived.

In my forever home, I've now created my own houseplant collection as a tribute to his legacy. Even if you don't have the space for a full garden, I highly recommend incorporating plants into your home decor. Tending to my plants helps calm my mind and soothe my anxieties, and I'm sure it can do the same for you. Whether you create a cozy houseplant nook or start a small container garden, I encourage you to make it a place of joy and tranquility where you can find solace in the beauty of nature.

Chapter 14

From Chaos to Calm

*Only when our greatest love is God, a
love that we cannot lose even in death,
can we face all things with peace.*

Timothy Keller, *Walking with God
through Pain and Suffering*

*T*he first time I experienced God's peace was in the back of the stranger's car, when I envisioned the altar of Jesus and felt his love wash over me. Since that life-changing moment, I've embarked on a journey to cultivate unshakable peace in my life. I've immersed myself in the wisdom of the Bible, sought guidance through talk therapies such as CBT, and delved into trauma therapies such as EMDR and IFS to clear the path to true, lasting peace. I no longer require perfect conditions to feel God's peace, but I can confidently approach God with open arms and receive his boundless love and tranquility. My heartfelt prayer is for your home to be a haven of peace where you can always take solace in his presence, no matter the chaos and challenges that life may bring.

In contrast to our conventional understanding of peace, true biblical peace is not conditional; it is not based on our circumstances. This means that in Christ, we can have peace, even when our external world is chaotic. Jesus said, "Peace I leave with you; my peace I give you" (John 14:27 NIV), and then he reassured his disciples that he was leaving behind a gift—peace of mind and heart.

This peace that Jesus offers is different from the peace offered by the world. The world's peace is dependent on external circumstances, but the peace that Jesus gives is steadfast and enduring. It cannot be taken away by any external situation. With this peace, we can have a sense of calm and well-being that goes beyond any temporary relief or solution that the world can offer.

In addition to the abiding peace you have in Jesus, you also have access to the Helper—the Holy Spirit. Jesus promised that the Holy Spirit would "teach you all things and will remind you of everything I [Jesus] have said to you" (John 14:26 NIV). The Holy Spirit is your divine Advocate, who will be with you to guide, comfort, and remind you of everything that Jesus wants you to know. With the Spirit ready to come to your aid, you can truly experience the peace that surpasses all understanding. Even in the midst of the most difficult circumstances, you can have a sense of peace that defies explanation. It is a peace that comes from knowing you are not alone, you are loved, and you have a source of strength and guidance that is greater than anything you can find in the world. So if you're feeling anxious or overwhelmed, take heart. Jesus offers you his peace, and the Holy Spirit is there to help you access it.

When I first joined my current church, it was a time of transition as the congregation had recently split from a long-standing megachurch and was working to establish their own unique culture and identity. Our community was made up of a diverse group of individuals from all walks of life, including young Korean American professionals, local university students, Hispanic families from the surrounding area, and people of other ethnicities, ages, and life stages. Despite the absence of a dedicated church building, all seven hundred of us gathered every Sunday under a tent at a nearby community college.

Our differences in culture and background did not hinder us; rather, these differences became a source of strength and vitality for our new church. The lack of a traditional church building and the unique mix of individuals made our Sundays feel like a real-life version of the Sermon on the Mount. I still remember the first-ever sermon series we heard in the tent, titled "23." It was an in-depth study of Psalm 23, the beloved psalm of King David. As a former shepherd, David had an intimate knowledge of sheep and pastures that allowed him to draw powerful analogies that spoke to our congregation on a deep level.

Psalm 23 begins with the powerful statement, "The LORD is my shepherd, I lack nothing" (Psalm 23:1 NIV). This is a bold affirmation of trust in God's provision and care. David compared himself to a sheep and God to a shepherd. He highlighted the vulnerability of sheep and their need for protection, care, and rest. Sheep cannot rest unless they know they are safe. In the presence of their good shepherd, they can lie down and rest beside quiet waters.

This analogy is relevant to us as we face our own vulnerabilities, fears, and anxieties. David recognized God as his trustworthy Master and found rest in his presence, free from worry about the presence of his enemies. The idea of a shepherd caring for their sheep was a powerful reminder of God's love and care for his people. This psalm laid the foundation of peace for our church, a diverse family of individuals from all walks of life. We gathered under that makeshift tent, bearing one another's burdens and praying for one another, because we shared a Shepherd who made us feel safe. His presence refreshed our souls and brought us peace.

Perhaps what you need in this season is to believe that you are protected by your Good Shepherd, Jesus Christ. With Jesus lovingly watching over you, you can breathe a sigh of relief and lie down in rest. I've found it helpful to memorize Psalm 23 to help me move away from anxiety and into God's peace. It reminds me that Jesus is a Shepherd who would die for his sheep. He is worthy of our trust, and we can place our confidence in him. I pray that as you lean on Jesus for your safety and protection, you will be filled with a deep, unwavering peace that can only come from him. Even though you may be walking through the darkest valley, I pray that his protection and guidance will comfort you.

May your cup overflow with the abundance of peace from being with your good and mighty Shepherd. In Jesus' name. Amen.

> Surely your goodness and love will follow me
> all the days of my life,
> and I will dwell in the house of the LORD
> forever.

Psalm 23:6 NIV

Design Your Wall of Peace

I invite you to create a gallery wall of calming words and paintings that convey peace. You can take a stroll through your local thrift shop for any frames, prints, or paintings that catch your eye and fit into the theme of peace. Psalm 23 is also incredibly descriptive and can provide wonderful inspiration for you while you stroll. Take this time to really be present, notice your body sensations, and enjoy looking at each row of unique items as you pass by.

Here is what I've found at my local thrift shop for this project:

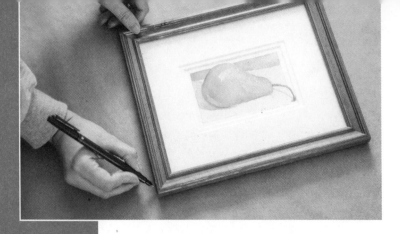

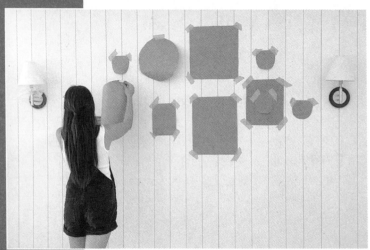

Step 1: Trace the Frames

Once you've found the total number of frames you want, trace them out on butcher paper (or wrapping paper).

Step 2: Cut and Arrange

Cut out your frames and arrange them on your wall with painter's tape until it looks right to you.

Step 3: Hang the Frames

Use the cutouts as guidelines for where to nail your frames. You can also use Command hooks for a renter-friendly option.

That's it! Now you can be reminded of the peace you've received from Jesus each time you walk by this gallery wall. I would love to see your creations, so please feel free to tag me on social media (@girlandtheword).

Chapter 15
The Wisdom of Joy and Suffering

Other people are going to find healing in your wounds. Your greatest life messages and your most effective ministry will come out of your deepest hurts.

Rick Warren, *The Purpose Driven Life*

*W*e know all too well that suffering is inevitable in this life. However, the beauty of our faith lies in the promise that God will not leave us unequipped or alone in our suffering. He has provided us with the Scriptures as a source of comfort and guidance, and he calls us to lean on one another for love and support. The fellowship of suffering can bring about the redemption of our pain and provide us with valuable lessons that we can use to help others. You may recall that this is known as posttraumatic growth or wisdom.

As I reflect on the wisdom gained from suffering, I'm reminded of the insight that Timothy Keller shared in *Walking with God through Pain and Suffering*: "While other worldviews lead us to sit in the midst of life's joys, foreseeing the coming sorrows, Christianity empowers its people to sit in the midst of this world's sorrows, tasting the coming joy."[1] This paradox is at the heart of the Christian faith. Through our suffering, we can gain a deeper understanding of ourselves, our faith, and our purpose. We learn to rely on God in ways we never thought possible and come to realize the strength and resilience he has given us. These hard-won lessons become valuable tools to equip us to minister to others who are going through similar trials.

When we share our stories and struggles with others, we can bring comfort, hope, and encouragement to those who are hurting. The apostle Paul understood this concept well: "[God] comforts us in all our troubles so that we can comfort others" (2 Corinthians 1:4). This cyclical pattern of loving others and sharing in one another's burdens is how we can get through even the most difficult times. The comfort we receive from the Lord can and should come from his people, and it will then become a source of empathy for us to share with those who are hurting in the same way.

So while we must sit in the midst of this world's sorrows, we can have hope in the promise of the fullness of joy we will one day experience when we meet Jesus face-to-face. Suffering can be a transformative experience that leads to the redemption of our pain and a deepened understanding of God's love and compassion.

It's important to note that while suffering can be a powerful teacher, it's not the only way to gain wisdom. There were moments in my life when I believed that my experiences of pain and hardship had taught me everything I needed to know. I remember discussing this with my dear friend Joanne,* who expressed her curiosity.

"Is it possible that it's pride?" she asked.

I took a moment to consider her question before replying, "It's interesting because intellectually I understand that I obviously don't know everything, but I think deep down, I believe that wisdom only comes through suffering. I just don't want to suffer anymore, even if it means missing out on more wisdom."

"I thought so," Joanne said, "but you should know that joy can also bring wisdom."

Leave it to Joanne to offer such a profound insight. I had never thought about joy as a source of wisdom before. Too often I've thought of suffering as the only way to gain wisdom, but there's much to be learned from joyful experiences as well. While it's true we often learn the most in difficult seasons, we can also gain wisdom from the incredible joy we find in Jesus.

When I experienced that divine hug in the back of the

---

* "Joanne" (pseud.).

stranger's car, I learned that there is truly a Creator who loves me deeply and knows me intimately. I gained the wisdom of his divine existence. When I moved into my own studio apartment for the first time, I learned to find my worth in what God thought of me instead of what my authority figures thought of me. I gained the wisdom of my true identity in Christ. When I walked into my forever home and was riddled by guilt, I learned that God wanted me to enjoy this beautiful gift from him. I gained the wisdom of receiving with grace and gratitude.

Wisdom can be gained from joyful celebrations and suffering alike. The key is to be attuned to God's presence during times of chaos and times of peace. We can cultivate this awareness by staying connected to him through prayer, meditation, and the study of his Word. In doing so, we open ourselves up to receive his guidance and wisdom for every experience we encounter. Through my journey, I have come to know that God is always eager to share his wisdom with us. It is up to us to remain open to his guidance and listen to his voice in our lives. When we do, we can gain the wisdom we need to navigate the challenges of life with grace and peace.

Design Your Box of Wisdom

I invite you to design your own box of wisdom where you can store all of the beautiful memories you've gained throughout the years—letters, journal entries, travel postcards, written prayers, photos, or any other life experience that is precious to you. When you look back on this box of wisdom and reflect on all of the ups and downs that he has brought you through, may you be empowered to keep walking alongside him through the hills and valleys.

Here are a few photos of what I've put inside my box of wisdom (otherwise known as my memory box). I keep this box in

my living room as shelf decor, so no one expects it to have such a profound function. I take it down and look through the tangible memories at least once every year, usually during Christmas. It never fails to remind me that life is profoundly worth living, even as I realize I didn't feel that way in some of those photos. God redeemed it all for my good and for his glory.

Congratulations on designing your life with the good gifts of the Father! Now it's time to truly live, and live well! With Christ as your rock-solid foundation, loving and supportive people surrounding you, and practical tools to help you regulate your emotions, you have everything you need to create a life that honors God and brings joy to your heart.

Even after applying the tools and strategies I've shared, you may still face challenges and fluctuations in your circumstances. Just like me, you may have to put in some ongoing effort to maintain your emotional well-being. But that's okay. The good news is that it is so worthwhile. When you're centered and secure in God's love, you can weather any storm that comes your way.

May I pray for you?

Dear heavenly Father, thank you for the wisdom and strength you offer in every season of life. As we walk with you on our healing journey, please help us to remain attuned to your presence, receive your guidance, and grow in wisdom from every experience we encounter. May we persevere through challenges with the assurance that you are with us, leading us on a path toward your Son, Jesus.

I pray that each person who reads these words will be empowered to design a life filled with your good gifts, surrounded by safe and supportive people, and equipped with the tools to maintain emotional soundness. May they find comfort and inspiration in the stories of others who have walked this path before them, and may they be encouraged to pursue a life of purpose and impact.

As we go forth, may we be ever mindful that you are always with us, comforting us and offering us guidance when we need it most. In Jesus' name. Amen.

Welcome to the Toolbox

Book Recommendations

Scan the QR code for my full list of book recommendations that helped me at each stage of my healing. I organized these references according to the chapters of this book. I pray that these texts will provide encouragement and insight as you build your forever home:

100 Emotions Word Bank

Below is a word bank of one hundred emotions to help you identify your complex emotions by category. My husband and I often refer to this word bank when we are too overwhelmed to make sense of our emotions. May it be a valuable asset in your toolbox!

HAPPY	SAD	ANGRY	CONFUSED	FEARFUL
Joyful	Despondent	Enraged	Perplexed	Terrified
Blissful	Disheartened	Furious	Bewildered	Panicked
Elated	Hopeless	Incensed	Baffled	Petrified
Euphoric	Dejected	Outraged	Puzzled	Horrified
Radiant	Despairing	Irate	Stumped	Alarmed
Delighted	Neglected	Livid	Mystified	Frightened
Thrilled	Miserable	Fuming	Discombobulated	Anxious
Ecstatic	Wretched	Seething	Dazed	Nervous
Grateful	Lonesome	Infuriated	Flustered	Uneasy
Jubilant	Sorrowful	Aggravated	Troubled	Dreadful
Overjoyed	Downcast	Wrathful	Unsettled	Scared
Enchanted	Gloomy	Resentful	Frustrated	Tense
Content	Sad	Vexed	Confused	Apprehensive
Cheerful	Melancholic	Annoyed	Mixed-up	Jittery
Amazed	Blue	Displeased	Unsure	Paralyzed
Excited	Joyless	Bitter	Uncertain	Shaken
Pleased	Unhappy	Hostile	Doubtful	Timid
Glad	Low-spirited	Indignant	Ambivalent	Hesitant
Exultant	Heartbroken	Out of control	Indecisive	Agitated
Gleeful	Distressed	Hateful	Hesitant	Wary

Soothing Techniques

Calming visualization. Create a mental image of a scene that relaxes you. This can be a secret beach you love visiting, the local plant nursery, or even your couch. Once you've picked a scene, notice all the details about it that are pleasant. My go-to scene is usually the secret beach in Malibu that I sneak off to on the weekend. When I'm feeling stressed or overwhelmed, I shut my eyes and envision walking toward 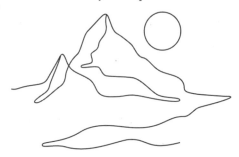 that Malibu beach. I notice how the cool, gentle breeze feels on my cheeks, and I imagine hearing seagulls flying far above. I make note of how the sun feels on my skin, the weight of my body, and every little detail about that specific moment until I'm ready to approach reality again. You can do the same with whichever scene feels the most comforting to you. Over time, the relaxing scene you create in your mind will become easier to rehearse whenever you feel overwhelmed. This is a wonderful technique to slow down your heart rate and expand your window of tolerance.

Box breathing. Breathe in through your nose for four counts, hold your breath for four counts, and breathe out through your mouth for four counts. You can repeat this however many times you need to feel more relaxed and regulated.

The container. Envision putting all of the things that bring you

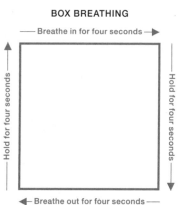

BOX BREATHING

Breathe in for four seconds →

Hold for four seconds

← Breathe out for four seconds —

anxiety inside a container and store it away for safekeeping. The goal is to give you reassurance that you can revisit this container at a later time. If you have trouble sleeping or concentrating on important tasks because of racing thoughts, envisioning the container will help you feel more at ease and in control of your mind.

Let's Invite Support

You shouldn't walk this path of healing alone. Find a group of safe people who can empathize with your pain and walk with you through it all. I've listed a variety of dependable contacts to accommodate different needs. Take a photo of this list so you can have it ready whenever you need it most:

- **Suicide and Crisis Lifeline (988):** The nation's comprehensive mental health crisis service
- **Blackline (1-800-604-5841):** A crisis hotline geared toward the Black, Indigenous, and People of Color communities
- **Wildflower Alliance (wildfloweralliance.org):** Peer-to-peer support, online support groups, free self-care classes, employment support
- **Kiva Centers (kivagroups.carrd.co):** Daily online peer support groups
- **Alcoholics Anonymous (aa.org):** Local support groups for those who struggle with alcoholism
- **Celebrate Recovery (celebraterecovery.com):** Regional support groups for anyone suffering from hurts, habits, and hang-ups

Acknowledgments

If not for Carolyn McCready, who saw my potential and gave me the opportunity to share my story with all of you, *Forever Home* would have just been a pipe dream. Thank you, Carolyn, for being my champion from the beginning. Your gentle guidance and nudging gave me the courage to share my vulnerable struggles in a way that could be of help to others. I am forever grateful for your unwavering support and belief in me.

Thank you also, Carolyn, for introducing me to Andrea Vinley Converse, who quickly became the older sister I needed throughout this writing process. Andrea, you have a way of honoring with such tender care and empathy every moment I shared. With your artistry, you captured the essence of my journey and brought it to life in a way that truly did it justice. Your mentorship has been a rare and precious gift, and I'm grateful to have created *Forever Home* with you. Please keep shining your light and know that your work is making a powerful impact in the lives of so many people.

Speaking of mentors, I also want to acknowledge Lysa TerKeurst and the Proverbs 31 ministry team for their profound influence on my writing process. Lysa, you have paved the way for a new generation of writers who strive to bring hope and healing through their storytelling. Your legacy is one of empowerment and inspiration for countless women who have followed in your footsteps, bravely sharing their own stories of pain and transformation. It has been a humbling privilege to be mentored by you and your team of brilliant thought leaders.

It would have been impossible to write this guidebook on healing without the extraordinary facilitator of healing, Kate DellaFera. Kate, God has truly used you to facilitate unimaginable levels of healing. I believed I knew myself before I entered your office, but it turned out that my understanding was quite shallow. Thank you for creating a safe space where I could confront painful memories and emerge victorious. You are a hero who saves lives every day.

I must also give my profoundest gratitude to my mother, Nguyet Nguyen, for graciously allowing me to tell my side of the story without reservations. I am constantly amazed by the depth of your love and your willingness to make changes for your only child. Despite our complex history, I find myself still aspiring to reach your level of generosity and bigheartedness toward others. You are a survivor and a picture of resilience. Thank you for equipping me with everything you possibly could, despite the suffering you endured. And finally, thank you for your ultimate demonstration of grace by helping me build my actual forever home. I am so proud and grateful to be your daughter.

Numerous individuals have accompanied me on my journey as an author and helped facilitate my healing over the years. Among those are the members of my small group, who taught me the true meaning of siblinghood in the church; Armen Karaoghlanian, who believed in me as a writer before anyone else; and my team at The Hooga Shop—Denisa Pavelkova, Ellie Sohn, and Eleanor Cho—who helped me share God's love and beauty with thousands of people online.

Regarding my healing journey, I must acknowledge Pastor Tom for creating the church culture of my dreams, Do Kim for curating spaces that open up hearts, Nilou Ajdari for being my confidante and soul sister, and Jonathan Lin for walking with me intimately throughout this entire process. You are my tribe.

Lastly, thank you to Dirk Buursma for thoughtfully editing each and every page of *Forever Home*. You took rough-sawn lumber and skillfully carved it into art. I am so inspired by your love for writing! Thank you also to Alicia Kasen, Meaghan Minkus, Bridgette Brooks, Devin Duke, Matt Bray, and Paul Fisher for lending me your marketing expertise and patiently guiding me through the promotional process. I am incredibly honored to work with so many kind and godly individuals from start to finish. May the prayers and hard work of every individual involved in bringing this book to life be felt in the transformative impact it has on your heart and life.

Notes

Chapter 1: The Beginning of My Healing Journey

1. Bessel A. van der Kolk, *The Body Keeps the Score: Brain, Mind, and Body in the Healing of Trauma* (New York: Penguin, 2015), 30.

2. See Center for Substance Abuse Treatment, "Understanding the Impact of Trauma," chapter 3 in *Trauma-Informed Care in Behavioral Health Services* (Rockville, MD: Substance Abuse and Mental Health Services Administration [US], 2014). Report no.: (SMA) 14-4816. PMID: 24901203, https://pubmed.ncbi.nlm.nih .gov/24901203.

3. See John Briere and Catherine Scott, "Complex Trauma in Adolescents and Adults: Effects and Treatment," *Psychiatric Clinics of North America* 38, no. 3 (September 2015): 515–27, https://pubmed.ncbi.nlm.nih.gov/26300036.

4. The catechism classes I attended typically covered topics from the Catechism of the Catholic Church (second edition, 1997), such as the Ten Commandments, the sacraments, and other core beliefs and practices of the Catholic Church. I was, of course, too young to understand any of it.

5. Van der Kolk, *Body Keeps the Score*, 29–30.

Chapter 2: You Are Loved

1. Henry Cloud and John Townsend, *Our Mothers, Ourselves* (Grand Rapids: Zondervan, 2015), 33.

2. See "Nurturing Care for Early Childhood Development," World Health Organization, May 18, 2018, www.who.int/teams /maternal-newborn-child-adolescent-health-and-ageing /child-health/nurturing-care.

3. See Robert Winston and Rebecca Chicot, "The Importance of Early Bonding on the Long-Term Mental Health and Resilience of Children," *London Journal of Primary Care* 8, no. 1 (February 2016): 12–14, www.ncbi.nlm.nih.gov/pmc/articles/PMC5330336.

4. Jude Cassidy, Jason D. Jones, and Phillip R. Shaver, "Contributions of Attachment Theory and Research: A Framework for Future Research, Translation, and Policy," *Development and Psychopathology* 25, no. 4, part 2 (November 2013): 1415–34, www.ncbi.nlm.nih.gov/pmc/articles /PMC4085672.

5. John Bowlby, *Attachment and Loss* (New York: Basic Books, 1969), 194.

6. See Morgan Mandriota, "Here Is How to Identify Your Attachment Style," PsychCentral, October 13, 2021, https:// psychcentral.com/health/4-attachment-styles-in-relationships.

7. See "Serve and Return," Center on the Developing Child, Harvard University, https://developingchild.harvard.edu/science /key-concepts/serve-and-return, accessed March 1, 2023.

8. Cited in Rachael A. Dansby Olufowote et al., "How Can I Become More Secure?: A Grounded Theory of Earning Secure Attachment," *Journal of Marital and Family Therapy* 46, no. 3 (July 2020): 489–506, https://doi.org/10.1111/jmft.12409.

9. See Olufowote et al., "How Can I Become More Secure?"

10. See Olufowote et al., "How Can I Become More Secure?"

11. See Olufowote et al., "How Can I Become More Secure?"

Chapter 3: Believing You Are Worthy

1. See Lois Zoppi, "What Is Trauma Bonding?" Medical News Today, November 26, 2020, www.medicalnewstoday.com /articles/trauma-bonding.

2. Doctor Ramani, "What Is 'Intimacy Avoidance'? (Glossary of

Narcissistic Relationships)," YouTube, April 27, 2020,
www.youtube.com/watch?v=30mNhZEow6s.

3. Bruce D. Perry and Oprah Winfrey, *What Happened to You? Conversations on Trauma, Resilience, and Healing* (New York: Flatiron, 2021), 22.

Chapter 4: Belonging in Your Tribe

1. Bruce D. Perry and Oprah Winfrey, *What Happened to You? Conversations on Trauma, Resilience, and Healing* (New York: Flatiron, 2021), 66.

2. Richard G. Tedeschi, "Growth after Trauma," *Harvard Business Review*, August 31, 2021, https://hbr.org/2020/07/growth-after -trauma.

Chapter 5: Becoming Who You Were Meant to Be

1. Amy Arnsten, Carolyn M. Mazure, and Rajita Sinha, "This Is Your Brain in Meltdown," *Scientific American* 306, no. 4 (April 2012): 48–53, www.ncbi.nlm.nih.gov/pmc/articles/PMC4774859.

2. See J. Douglas Bremner, "Traumatic Stress: Effects on the Brain," *Dialogues in Clinical Neuroscience* 8, no. 4 (December 2006): 445–61, www.ncbi.nlm.nih.gov/pmc/articles/PMC3181836.

3. See Daniel Preiato and Ryan Collins, "Exercise and the Brain: The Mental Health Benefits of Exercise," Healthline, January 31, 2022, www.healthline.com/health/depression/exercise.

Chapter 6: Strengthening Your Boundaries

1. See Henry Cloud and John Townsend, *Boundaries: When to Say Yes, When to Say No to Take Control of Your Life* (Grand Rapids: Zondervan, 1992), 32.

2. Henry Cloud and John Townsend, *Boundaries with Kids: When to Say Yes, When to Say No to Help Your Children Take Control of Their Lives* (Grand Rapids: Zondervan, 1998), 72.

3. Henry Cloud, *Changes That Heal: Four Practical Steps to a Happier, Healthier You* (Grand Rapids: Zondervan, 2018), 136.

4. Cloud, *Changes That Heal*, 136.

Chapter 7: Shielded by Grace

1. See Shuya Yan et al., "The Effectiveness of Eye Movement Desensitization and Reprocessing toward Adults with Major Depressive Disorder: A Meta-Analysis of Randomized Controlled Trials," *Frontiers in Psychiatry* 12 (August 2021), www.frontiersin .org/articles/10.3389/fpsyt.2021.700458/full; Liuva Capezzani et al., "EMDR and CBT for Cancer Patients: Comparative Study of Effects on PTSD, Anxiety, and Depression," *Journal of EMDR Practice and Research* 7, no. 3 (January 2013), https:// connect.springerpub.com/content/sgremdr/7/3/134.abstract; Hwallip Bae et al., "Add-on Eye Movement Desensitization and Reprocessing (EMDR) Therapy for Adults with Post-traumatic Stress Disorder Who Failed to Respond to Initial Antidepressant Pharmacotherapy," *Journal of Korean Medical Science* 33, no. 48 (November 2018), www.ncbi.nlm.nih.gov/pmc/articles /PMC6249165.
2. Francine Shapiro, *Eye Movement Desensitization and Reprocessing (EMDR) Therapy: Basic Principles, Protocols, and Procedures*, 3rd ed. (New York: Guilford, 2018), 7.
3. See "Eye Movement Desensitization and Reprocessing (EMDR) Therapy," American Psychological Association, www.apa.org /ptsd-guideline/treatments/eye-movement-reprocessing, accessed March 15, 2023.
4. Bessel A. van der Kolk, *The Body Keeps the Score: Brain, Mind, and Body in the Healing of Trauma* (New York: Penguin, 2015), 262.
5. van der Kolk, *Body Keeps the Score*, 261–62.
6. Rick Warren, *The Purpose Driven Life: What on Earth Am I Here For?* (Grand Rapids: Zondervan, 2002), 29.
7. Timothy Keller, *Walking with God through Pain and Suffering* (New York: Penguin, 2016), 284.

Chapter 8: The Power of Perspective

1. See Benjamin Hardy, "One Technique for Reframing Traumatic Memories," *Psychology Today*, February 6, 2020,

www.psychologytoday.com/us/blog/quantum-leaps/202002
/one-technique-reframing-traumatic-memories.

2. "Peter Levine on Working with Memory to Reframe a Traumatic Experience," YouTube, www.youtube.com/watch?v=KIC8hUrQbV8, accessed March 15, 2023.

3. See Ayesh Perera, "Framing Effect in Psychology," SimplyPsychology, February 8, 2023, www.simplypsychology.org/framing-effect.html.

4. Timothy Keller, *Walking with God through Pain and Suffering* (New York: Penguin, 2016), 308.

Chapter 9: Strategies for Endurance

1. Angela Duckworth, *Grit: The Power of Passion and Perseverance* (New York: Scribner, 2018), 269.

2. "FAQ," Angela Duckworth, https://angeladuckworth.com/qa, accessed March 15, 2023.

3. Quoted in "Pastor Rick Warren Says His Son Committed Suicide," CBS Sacramento, April 7, 2013, www.cbsnews.com /sacramento/news/pastor-rick-warren-says-his-son-committed -suicide.

4. Rick Warren, "The Most Important Interview I've Ever Done," Pastors.com, September 18, 2013, https://pastors.com/piers.

5. "How We're Getting Through," introduction to sermon series "How to Get Through What You're Going Through," Saddleback Church (July–September 2013), https://saddleback.com/watch /how-to-get-through-what-youre-going-through/how-were -getting-through.

6. "How We're Getting Through."

7. Warren, "Most Important Interview."

8. "How We're Getting Through."

Chapter 11: Cultivating Godly Mindfulness

1. Gabor Maté, *In the Realm of Hungry Ghosts: Close Encounters with Addiction* (Berkeley, CA: North Atlantic, 2008), 38.

2. See Richard C. Schwartz, *No Bad Parts: Healing Trauma and Restoring Wholeness with the Internal Family Systems Model* (Boulder, CO: Sounds True, 2021), 103.

3. Schwartz, *No Bad Parts*, 27.

Chapter 12: Forgiving the Unforgivable

1. *The Jesus Bible, NIV Edition* (Grand Rapids: Zondervan, 2017), 777.

Chapter 15: The Wisdom of Joy and Suffering

1. Timothy Keller, *Walking with God through Pain and Suffering* (New York: Penguin, 2016), 31.